EXPLORE THE WORLD

CYPRUS

Author:
Waldemar Weiß

*An Up-to-date travel guide
with 41 color photos
and 10 maps*

NELLES

IMPRINT / LEGEND

Dear Reader: Being up-to-date is the main goal of the Nelles series. Our correspondents help keep us abreast of the latest developments in the travel scene, while our cartographers see to it that maps are also kept completely current. However, as the travel world is constantly changing, we cannot guarantee that all the information contained in our books is always valid. Should you come across a discrepancy, please contact us at: Nelles Verlag, Schleissheimer Str. 371 b, 80935 Munich, Germany, tel. (089) 3571940, fax. (089) 35719430, e-mail: Nelles.Verlag@t-online.de

Note: Distances and measurements, including temperatures, used in this guide are metric. For conversion information, please see the *Guidelines* section of this book.

LEGEND

★★	Main Attraction *(on map)*	
★★	*(in text)*	
★	Worth Seeing *(on map)*	
★	*(in text)*	
❽	Orientation Number in Text and on Map	
▪	Public or Significant Building	
▪	Hotel	
▪	Shopping Center / Market	
✝	Church	
☾	Mosque	

Larnaca *(Town)* / Church *(Sight)* — Places Highlighted in Yellow Appear in Text

✈ ✈ — International Airport / National Airport

Khionistra • (1612) — Mountain (altitude in meters)

\ 13 / — Distance in Kilometers

✳ — Beach

Ⓢ Ⓢ Ⓢ — Luxury Hotel Category
Ⓢ Ⓢ — Moderate Hotel Category
Ⓢ — Budget Hotel Category
(for price information see "Accomodation" in Guidelines section)

▨▨▨	Line of Demarcation
═══	Expressway
━━━	Principal Highway
────	Main Road
────	Provincial Road
────	Secondary Road
+++++	Road closed to Traffic
① ②	Route Number
⛴	Ferry
⊤	Lighthouse
⸫	Ancient Site

CYPRUS
© Nelles Verlag GmbH, 80935 Munich
    All rights reserved

First Edition 2001
ISBN 3-88618-732-2 (Nelles Travel Pack)
ISBN 3-88618-772-1 (Nelles Pocket)
Printed in Slovenia

Publisher:	Günter Nelles	**Cartography:**	Nelles Verlag GmbH
Managing Editor:	Berthold Schwarz	**Color Separation:**	Priegnitz, Munich
English Edition Editor:	Kerstin Borch	**Printed by:**	Gorenjski Tisk

                                                                                                    - S07 -

TABLE OF CONTENTS

GUIDELINES

LIST OF MAPS

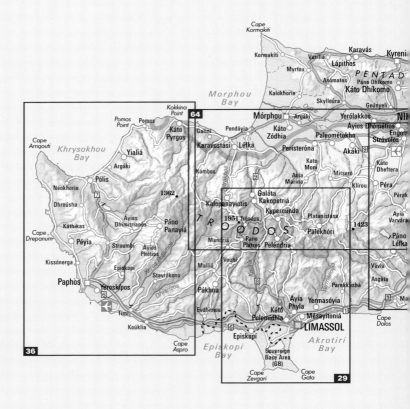

M E D I T E R R A N E A N

S E A

CYPRUS

0   10   20 km

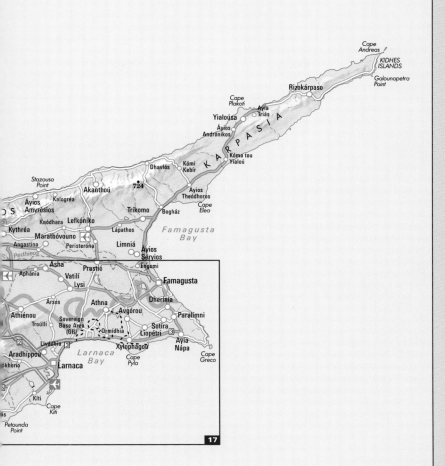

Cape
Andreas

KIDHES
ISLANDS

Galounopetra
Point

Rizokárpaso

Cape
Plakoti
Yialoúsa   Ayía
Triás
Áyios
Andrónikos

K A R P A S I A

Kóma tou
Yíaloú

Dhavlós   Kómi
Kebír

Stazousa
Point
Akanthoú   724   Áyios
Theódhoros
Áyios   Kalogréa   Cape
Amyrósios   Elea
Trikomo   Boghaz
Knódhara   Lefkóniko
Kythréa   Lápathos   Famagusta
Marathóvouno   Bay
Angastina   Limniá
Peristeróna   Áyios
pedhieos   Sérvios
Asha   Éngomi
Aphánia   Prastió
Vatilí   Famagusta
Lysi
Ársos   Dherínia
Athiénou   Athna   Avgórou   Paralími
Troúlli   Sovereign   Sotíra
Base Area   Ormidhia   Liopétri
(GB)   Ayía
Livádhia   Nápa
Aradhíppou   Xylophágou   Cape
Larnaca   Greco
Bay   Cape
Pyla
Kíti   Larnaca

Cape
Kíti
Petounda
Point

17

M E D I T E R R A N E A N

S E A

EARLY HISTORY

Ca. 9000 B.C. Skeletal findings show that the island was once colonized by dwarf species of hippos and elephants, chased to their deaths over the steep cliffs of the Akrotiri Peninsula by man, thus being forced into extinction.

7000-6000 B.C. Early Stone Age farmers build the round mud and stone houses of Khirokitia. They bury their dead beneath the floors of their houses.

4500-3800 B.C. Neolithic settlement in southern Sotira. It is the people of Sotira who manufactured the so-called combed pottery.

3800-2500 B.C. Burials begin to take place outside the settlements (e.g. Lemba). Copper jewelry and tools are important burial objects to accompany the dead, as are both masculine and feminine icon figurines with outstretched arms in the shape of a cross. Findings from Obsidian reveal links with Anatolia.

2500-1900 B.C. Bronze production becomes widespread relatively late, and largely due to immigrants from Asia Minor; this is confirmed by findings in the region around Kyrenia (Girne) in northern Cyprus.

1900-1600 B.C. City kingdoms such as Enkomi, Lapithos (both northern Cyprus) and Kition come into being.

1600-1250 B.C. Mainland Greeks (Mycenaeans) and Cretans introduce their script, from which Cypro-Minoan script developed, which remains undeciphered. Paleokastro-Maa becomes a Mycenaean center, but only for a short time.

From 1250 B.C. Settled Mycenaeans are driven out by Dorians. Kition and Enkomi are destroyed by unknown invaders.

ANTIQUITY

Ca. 1050 B.C. A heavy earthquake destroys almost all of the Bronze Age settlements on Cyprus.

950-333 B.C. Phoenicians, Assyrians, Egyptians and Persians, in succession, conquer the island. A Cypriot fleet supports the Persians - **480 B.C.** – without success – in the *Naval Battle of Salamis* against the Athenians.

Hellenistic-Roman Era:

333 B.C. Cypriot Kings form an alliance with Alexander the Great.

294-58 B.C. The Ptolemies, who assume control of Egypt in succession to Alexander, conquer Cyprus and Nikokreon of Salamis becomes the sole ruler of the island. The link with Egypt leads to a commercial upswing. Hellenistic Ptolemies are mainly interested in the island's copper, cereals and wood for ship-building. (Nea) Paphos is replaced by Salamis as the capital city.

58 B.C.-395 A.D. The Romans conquer Cyprus. Most of the ancient buildings on the island date from the period of their rule.

45 A.D. Paul the Apostle and Barnabas set up missions in Paphos and Salamis. But despite Cyprus being the first country under Christian rule, Chris-

Such Bronze Age bull portrayals lead one to assume that a fertility cult once existed on Cyprus (clay model, Cyprus Museum, Nicosia).

tianity made very little progress here until the 4th century.

BYZANTINE-ARABIAN PERIOD

395 Cyprus falls into the hands of Byzantium when the Roman Empire is split.

342 After a severe earthquake, Salamis, now known as *Constantia*, becomes the capital city once again, confirming the decline of Nea Paphos.

647-965 The island is repeatedly attacked by Arabs. Thousands of Christians are either murdered or enslaved.

965 The Byzantine Emperor Nikephoros II Phokas reconquers Cyprus.

FRANCO-VENETIAN PERIOD

1191 Richard the Lionheart conquers the island and leaves it to the Knights Templar.

1192-1489 Under the absolutist rule of the Lusignan Dynasty, Roman Catholicism becomes the official

A glance into the UN buffer zone behind the demarcation line in Nicosia - the Green Line, dividing Cyprus' capital city since 1964.

religion. Cyprus becomes a strategic base for the crusades in the Holy Land.

1489-1571 After the death of Jacques II "of Cyprus, Armenia and Jerusalem," Queen Caterina, his Venetian widow, abdicates. Cyprus falls to Venice.

OTTOMAN-BRITISH PERIOD

1571-1878 After conquering the island, the Turks abolish serfdom, grant the Cypriots their own Arch-

bishop and convert the catholic churches into mosques. For the first time, the island is colonized by Turks. A particular phenomenon of this era are the *linobambakoi*, Greek-Orthodox or Catholic Christians, who convert to Islam in order to pay less taxes.

1878 The Ottoman Empire „leases" Cyprus to the superpower of Great Britain.

1914 When the Turks join the Central Powers in the Great War, the British annex the island and in **1925** declare it a crown colony.

1931 Greek-Cypriot supporters of the *Enosis* movement demand the unification of Cyprus with Greece. The British manage to suppress this revolt, aided by Egyptian forces.

1948 For the first time the Turkish-Cypriot National Party - *Kibris Türktür* - demands that upon British withdrawal, Cyprus must be handed over to Turkey, or the island must be divided.

1950 In a referendum led by Archbishop Makarios III, 96 % of Greek Cypriots vote for unification with Greece.

From 1955 The military wing of the *Enosis* movement, the EOKA, launches attacks on the British, in an attempt to bring about unification by force.

INDEPENDENCE AND DIVISION

1960 Greece, Great Britain and Turkey declare Cyprus a sovereign state.

1963 Makarios III, first President of Cyprus, plans a constitutional amendment, which the Turkish Cypriots perceive as threatening their constitutional rights. Fights with the Greek population ensue.

1964 UN peacekeeping forces are deployed on the island. British officers draw a cease-fire line across Nicosia, known as the *Green Line*.

1974 After a coup against Makarios, organized by the Athens junta, Turkish troops annex the northern part of Cyprus (37 % of the country). The *Green Line* now extends from Kokkina in the northwest to Famagusta, 180 km to the east.

1977 Death of President Makarios.

1983 Turkish Cypriots proclaim the Turkish zone as the „Turkish Republic of Northern Cyprus" - not recognized by any country other than Turkey.

Since 1994 Southern Cyprus enters into negotiations to join the EU, despite threats from Northern Cyprus to definitively unite with Turkey.

THE GATEWAY TO CYPRUS

LARNACA
WEST OF LARNACA
NORTHEAST OF LARNACA
FAMAGUSTA DISTRICT

LARNACA

Once a quiet seaside village, **Larnaca** ❶ (Greek: *Lárnaka)* is today a major tourist center and a booming city bustling with activity. After the partition of the island in 1974 and the closure of Nicosia International Airport, Larnaca Airport was expanded to become the major international entry point on the island. The population has more than tripled in the last 20 years and continues to expand into outlying areas. The marina directly on the main waterfront is well developed. It offers more than 400 berths in the summertime, and year-round sailors like to spend the winter in its well-protected harbor.

Much of modern-day Larnaca has been built over the site of ancient *Kition*, a city dating from the 13th century B.C., when it was inhabited by Mycenaeans, who traded here. Larnaca succeeded Kition, some say it took its name from the ancient tombs and urns, in Greek the *larnax*, on which it was built. Raided by invaders and crippled by a powerful earthquake, the city of Kition disappeared during the

Preceding pages: Aphrodite, the Goddess of Love, who rose from the sea before Cyprus. Coral Bay on the west coast - the most beautiful beach in all of Paphos District. Left: Richly adorned iconostasis in Kato Lefkara.

Dark Ages that encompassed the entire eastern Mediterranean, only to re-emerge centuries later as a Phoenician town with strong links to the city of Tyre, in what is now Lebanon. It remained an important city right up to the seventh century A.D., when it was persistently destroyed in a succession of Arab raids.

Zeno the Stoic, who founded the ancient school of Stoic philosophy in Athens, is the city's most famous native son. Lazarus, who according to the Bible was raised from the dead by Jesus, is said to have lived his second life here, after being expelled from the Holy Land by the Jews. According to tradition, he lived another 30 years before dying again, and was consecrated as the first Bishop of Kition. Larnaca still remembers the holy man and annually, on the evening before Palm Sunday, a procession with his icon starts from the Church of Ayios Lazaros.

From 1683 onwards and thanks to many foreign consulates setting up their offices here, Larnaca became a diplomatic center. During the Ottoman occupation and the early days of British colonial rule, it was also an important trade center. These activities lent Larnaca a "continental" flavor, and it has been estimated that in 1816 about 1,000 Europeans lived here, quite a remarkable number for the time.

LARNACA

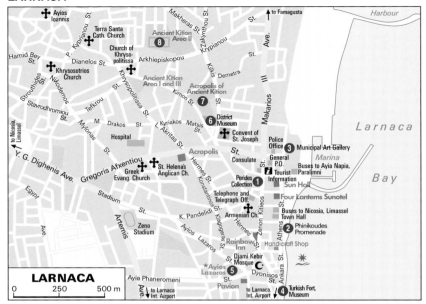

Colorful members of the diplomatic corps included General Luigi Palma di Cesnola, appointed American consul in 1865. At the same time, he was also the Russian consul. He was an archeology buff of dubious reputation who immediately set about excavating extensively at ancient sites all over the island, generally undisturbed by the indifferent Turkish authorities. A dazzling collection of silver and gold, supposedly from Kourion, was discovered by Cesnola and sold to the Metropolitan Museum in New York. Only at Ormidhia, outside the jurisdiction of Larnaca, was it possible to take formal action against him in the courts, and he had to return his findings.

In the 1840s, the importance of Larnaca was overshadowed by the successful maritime cities of Famagusta and Limassol. But the invasion of the island by the Turkish army proved to be a turn-

Right: Larnaca's promenade between the marina and the Turkish Fortress, better known as "Phinikoudes".

ing point in the city's history. Refugees from the 1974 invasion swelled its population, which is now estimated at around 60,000. Its port was enlarged, but more importantly for the city, an old airport runway to its south was hastily repaired and a new terminal set up to meet urgent air traffic requirements after the closure of Nicosia International Airport. Nicosia Airport, today in the no man's land between the island's divided communities, is now used only by the UN peace-keeping force which mans a buffer zone along the island's *Green Line*.

Getting Around

The **Pierides Foundation** ❶, the most important privately owned collection of Cypriot antiquities, can be found in Zenon Kitieos Street. The Pierides Collection was mostly gathered by scholar and archeologist Demetrios Pierides (1811-1895) and his family. Pottery of different periods comprises part of the collection of over 2,500 pieces.

14   **Info pp. 22-23**

The most popular place for a stroll, and indeed the place to be seen, is the more than 70 year-old palm tree-lined promenade between the Marina and the Turkish Fort, known as **Phinikoudes ❷**, with its many restaurants and outdoor cafés. At its northern end, housed in two former warehouse buildings from the late 19th century, is the **Municipal Art Gallery ❸** on modern Europe Square. Here, the works of mostly 20th century Cypriot artists are temporarily exhibited. Right next door, the **Museum of Paleontology** presents exhibits of fossils from all over the world.

Moving south, right to the end of Athens Street, you will come directly to the old **Turkish Fortress ❹**. It was built in 1625 to defend the town, and it later served as a prison and observation post for the port. It was also used as a prison by the British during the early part of their rule, before they turned it into the police headquarters. The Turkish Fortress is presently a **Museum**, which houses some exhibits from Kition.

West of the fortress lies the distinctive ★**Church of Ayios Lazaros ❺**, one of Larnaca's oldest monuments, which has a fascinating history. It was built around A.D. 900 by the Byzantine Emperor Leo VI, over what was supposed to have been the empty grave of Lazarus. Lazarus probably traveled more after his (second) death than he had done during his lifetime. His body is said to have been transported from Kition first to Constantinople, and then to its final resting place in Marseilles. The tomb, probably discovered in the year 890, bears the Greek inscription: "Lazarus, friend of Christ." Although very little now remains of the ninth century building, it had been rebuilt in the 17th century in accordance with its original design and was later embellished with an impressive bell tower, one of the very few permitted by the Turks before 1857. Inside the church, the iconostasis, or wooden screen with icons, between the altar and the parish room, displays some of the island's most remarkable 18th century carvings. Beneath the altar floor is the marble sarcophagus which is believed to have been the tomb of Lazarus.

The modern **District Museum** ❻ exhibits an interesting collection of prehistoric and ancient findings from the District of Larnaca, dating from the Neolithic to the Roman Periods. The well-displayed findings also feature items from Kition, including a ceramic collection with graceful alabaster vases, tools, coins and lamps. Also notable are Mycenaean *kraters* (mixing jugs) and an ivory figure of the ungainly Egyptian dwarf-god Bes. Wall cases also hold many significant pieces, which illustrate the area's history, including faience scarabs, limestone and cylindrical seals, as well as tools made of bone and engraved stone slabs from Khirokitia.

To the northwest of the District Museum, further along Kimon Street, on the right-hand side of the road lie the amorphous ruins of the **Acropolis** ❼ of the ancient city of Kition, a region today known as *Bamboula*.

Further to the north, you will arrive at the entrance to the most important archaeological site in all of ancient Kition, known as Area II ❽. On the premises are the remains of a total of five holy temples, including a Phoenician **Temple of Astarte**, which had been built over the ruins of an earlier Bronze Age temple. Part of the previous northern city walls can also be viewed, with the lower sections built of huge stone blocks resembling Mycenaean cyclopean walls. Extremely little remains of the Hellenistic Period that followed, and practically nothing at all of the subsequent Roman Period.

Quantities of copper slag and evidence of copper-smelting workshops have been discovered, which date back to the beginning of the 13th century B.C. A large cache of ivory objects discovered in a room of the Holy of Holies includes a plaque with the Egyptian god Bes and a pipe, which was perhaps used to smoke opium. All of these pieces bear inscrip-

tions in the as yet undeciphered Cypro-Minoan script of the Late Bronze Age. The city of Kition was re-inhabited and rebuilt on a larger scale in about 1200 B.C. Based on the evidence found, these new inhabitants were refugees from the main centers of the Peloponnese.

SOUTHWEST OF LARNACA

When heading out of Larnaca in a southerly direction, its Salt Lake stretches out on the right-hand side. During the winter months this lake fills up with seawater and becomes a temporary habitat for flamingos, herons and swans. In summertime, the lake dries up completely and tranforms into a salt pan.

Larnaca

LARNACA DISTRICT

0   5   10 km

Beyond the lake, a right turn will bring you to the **★★Hala Sultan Tekke ❷**, one of the most significant Moslem shrines. It attracts many pilgrims, especially on the religious holidays of *Shekir Bayram* and *Kurban Bayram*, and houses the tomb of Umm Haram, an aunt of the Prophet Mohammed. As the wife of the governor of Palestine, she was part of the Sultan's entourage during the expedition to Cyprus in 647 under Caliph Oman. She allegedly died here after falling from her mule. Surrounded by the buildings of a former dervish monastery (Turkish: *tekke*), the octagonal mosque with a minaret was built in 1816 over the site of Umm Haram's grave. Three stones, supposedly from Mount Sinai, mark her tomb; one of these

is said to have miraculously suspended itself in the air for many centuries.

About 11 kilometers southwest of Larnaca is the village of **Kiti ❸**, famous for its **Church of Panayia Angeloktisti**, the latter word meaning "built by angels." The church contains an outstanding mosaic that is thought to date back to about the fifth century. This masterpiece decorates the apse and depicts the *Virgin Mary flanked by the Archangels Gabriel and Michael*.

A small **lighthouse**, dating from 1864, rises up on **Cape Kiti**. North of the lighthouse is a **Venetian Watchtower ❹**, a solitary medieval monument. The tower itself is closed, but the Venetian coat of arms, the Lion of St. Mark, is still visible.

WEST OF LARNACA

One of the main attractions in the western part of Larnaca District is the monastery on Stavrovouni, the "Mountain of the Cross." It can be reached from the main Nicosia-Limassol highway.

First the road passes the **Aqueduct of Larnaca ❺**, called *Kamares*, the Greek word for "arches." Built in 1746 by Bekir Pasha, a wealthy Turkish governor of Cyprus, it supplied fresh water to the city of Larnaca for almost 200 years. The water was carried along open channels over the 75 arches of the aqueduct.

Off the highway, follow the road through the villages of Kalokhorio and Ayia Anna to **Pyrga ❻**, a charming little village amid many olive and carob trees. When entering the village you'll see **Ayia Marina**, a little domed 15th century cha-

Above: The Hala Sultan Tekke, an important Moslem shrine situated at Larnaca's Salt Lake. Right: Kato Lefkara, nestled in the foothills of the Troodos Mountains.

pel in which fragments of paintings survive. One of the outstanding examples of Lusignan architecture is the little stone chapel of **Ayia Katherina**, known as the *Chapelle Royale*. It was built in 1421, probably by Lusignan King Janus. In the outstanding fresco *The Crucifixion* in the west end of the chapel, he is pictured with his second wife, Charlotte de Bourbon. Other frescoes in the chapel, such as *The Last Supper* and *The Raising of Lazarus*, bear French inscriptions.

Stavrovouni Monastery

The **Ayia Varvara Monastery ❼** is a dependency of Stavrovouni Monastery. Until recently, the fields and gardens of this hilltop monastery were cultivated. The buildings date from the 18th century, and a noteworthy botanical feature of the monastery's gardens is the cultivation of the lotus plant. But the monks here also sell olive oil and honey, and one of them, a painter, offers his works of art for sale in his studio opposite the entrance.

The **Stavrovouni Monastery** ❽, 6.5 km further and considered the oldest in Cyprus, commands spectacular views of the Troodos Mountains, the southeast of the island and the sea, from its perch on a rocky peak. While women are not allowed inside the facility, the view from here is so terrific that this in itself is reason enough for making the trip. The peak, over 600 meters in height, was known in ancient times as Olympos, and was adorned by a temple to the goddess Aphrodite. According to tradition, it was claimed in the name of Christianity by Empress Helena, the mother of Constantine the Great. She is said to have founded the monastery in A.D. 327 in order to protect one of the fragments of the Holy Cross which she had brought with her from Jerusalem. Hence the name of the monastery: Stavrovouni means "Mountain of the Cross." This was one of the most important Christian sites of pilgrimage from earliest times.

This monastery was destroyed many times over the centuries, by Saracen raiders in 1426, an earthquake in 1492 and by the Turks in 1570, who burnt it to the ground. They are said to have carried away a solid gold cross with their captured booty. The rebuilt monastery as it is now stands, dates from the 17th and 18th centuries. Only the foundations - great stone blocks, are reminders of the original structure.

Lefkara

Lefkara, split into **Pano Lefkara** ❾ and the smaller **Kato Lefkara**, is a picturesque village nestled in the foohills of the Troodos Mountains. it is famous for its handmade lace, known as *lefkaritika*, a local specialty produced here since the Middle Ages. It is said that Leonardo da Vinci, whilst visiting the island, bought lace here for the altar cloth of the Cathedral of Milan, although skeptics claim he never once set foot on the island of Cyprus. Indeed, there are some people who claim the term "lace" is incorrect and that it is actually nothing more than embroidery on linen. Nevertheless, it is lovely to look at and a source of business for the women of Lefkara, who can be seen clustered in busy groups in the narrow village lanes, intently embroidering intricate geometric patterns. In the village there are also skilled silversmiths who create fine filigree work, as well as a small business producing Turkish Delight (Greek: *loukoumi*). In any event, a visit must be made to the **Folkloric Museum** in the restored Patsalos House. The museum shows what life was like on the island of Cyprus a hundred years ago. The household furnishings of a wealthy family of that time are on exhibit, as well as local traditional costumes and, of course, examples of lacework. Vacationers traveling by car can make a detour to the **Ayios Minas Monastery**, where a number of nuns paint splendid icons.

*Khirokitia

Further south lies ***Khirokitia ⑩**, one of the oldest Neolithic sites on the island (on most of the newer road signs it is spelled Choirokoitia). It probably dates from between 7000 and 6000 B.C. Settlers were farmers who cultivated wheat and barley, judging from flint sickle blades and analysis of carbonized seed material. The bones of animals found here also provide evidence of early livestock breeding as well as hunting. Fragments of pottery have been unearthed from a later period of settlement around 3500 B.C. The findings from Khirokitia can be viewed in the Cyprus Museum in Nicosia.

The archeological site is close to the dry Maroni riverbed. It is situated atop a hill, once covered in dense vegetation. When first excavated in 1934, a succession of *tholoi*, or beehive-shaped houses of single round rooms made of mud and

stone, were unearthed. The houses were all equipped with hearths, benches and tables. Beneath the floors, the dead were buried in a squatting position, with their knees drawn up to their chins. Apparently each hut that fell into disrepair was flattened, forming the foundation for a new one which was erected on top of it. In one hut there is evidence of 26 burials under eight superimposed layers of floor. A good idea of what these houses would have looked like is provided by the reconstruction of four of them, which can also be entered.

Another Neolithic settlement, that of **Kalavasos-Tenta ⑪**, lies southwest of Khirokitia and is worth seeing. Perhaps its most interesting finding, a depiction of a human figure etched in red paint, is the oldest two-dimensional portrayal discovered on Cyprus and is estimated to be over 5,000 years old. It is now on display in the Cyprus Museum in Nicosia.

NORTHEAST OF LARNACA

Drive along the coast road three kilometers northeast of Larnaca past the town of Livadhia. About two kilometers after that a left fork leads to **Voroklini ⑫**, which, like Livadhia, is a center of basket-weaving. Nowadays however, this craft is only practiced by a few of the older residents. Those interested in French literature might like to visit a nearby abandoned quarry, where the French poet Arthur Rimbaud worked in the winter of 1878/79. Another two kilometers further, a road bearing left leads to **Pyla ⑬**, situated in the UN-controlled buffer zone and inhabited by both Greek and Turkish Cypriots. In the harmonious hamlet of 700 Greek and 400 Turkish Cypriots, shops sell international textiles and other goods duty free. However, a word of caution when shopping: it is illegal to buy from Turkish shops, and purchased goods may be confiscated by the authorities.

Right: Beautiful relievo work on a marble fountain in the square of the Ayia Napa Monastery.

Next you pass the extraterritorial British military base of **Dhekelia** ⑭, a remnant of the days of colonial rule.

FAMAGUSTA DISTRICT

The Famagusta area, northeast of Larnaca, is famed for its beautiful beaches and clear waters. It lies partly in the southern Republic and is one of the most popular tourist destinations on the island.

About three kilometers out of **Xylophagou**, a right turn leads you to **Potamos** ⑮, at the mouth of a river, where innumerable small fishing vessels are moored. Two simple tavernas here serve good and inexpensive fish dishes. The small modern chapel of **Ayia Thekla** ⑯ is situated beside the road, six kilometers before Ayia Napa, and lies near a small sandy beach of the same name. From here, a string of magnificent beaches continues almost as far as the rocky headland of Cape Greco in the east, and then picks up again past the cape

along the southeastern coast of **Famagusta Bay**.

On the **Makronissos Peninsula** ⑰, 19 **rock tombs** from Roman and Hellenic times can be seen about 250 meters east of Hotel Dome. Beyond this lie the famous beaches of **Golden Sands** and **Nissi Bay.**

Ayia Napa ⑱ doesn't have too many sights to speak of, but it does offer numerous recreational activities to compensate for this. For example, there is an aquatic center with a giant water slide, a "dolphinarium," the fair-style Luna Park, and even a place to go bungee jumping. Anyone interested in sea shells can check out the small **Malacology Museum** in the Town Hall.

Also worth a look is the modern main church of Ayia Napa, dedicated to St. Mary. It has traditional Byzantine murals and stands on a broad square below the only historically interesting building in town, the **Ayia Napa Monastery**. It was erected about 1530 by Venetian nobles around an early cave church from the 8th or 9th century. Now it serves as an ecumenical meeting place for Christians in the Near East. A beautiful octagonal fountain, with relief sculptures, graces the center of the courtyard. The giant sycamore outside the south gate is over 600 years old and stands some 24 meters tall.

Beaches on the far side of Cape Greco can be accessed through Paralimni, but the slightly more strenuous coastal drive along rocky cape **Cape Greco** ⑲ is well worth the effort. The tip of the cape, now a protected area, is dominated by an austere radio transmitter mast, standing on a spot which in antiquity was devoted to Aphrodite. Unfortunately, the narrow winding road that leads to the cape's tip is blocked off to traffic shortly before its end.

The main beaches of Famagusta Bay are around **Protaras** ⑳, of which **Fig Tree Bay** is the most famous, taking its name from a mature fig tree that is a well-known landmark. Adjoining Fig Tree Bay are **Flamingo Bay** and shallow **Pernera Bay**, and somewhat further up the coast lies **Kalamies**. Not far off the main road between Protaras and Paralimni is the **Church of Ayios Ilias** ㉑, sitting on a rocky outcrop. The church itself is modern and not especially remarkable, but the view from here is lovely.

North of Paralimni is the village of **Dherinia** ㉒, with three 15th to 17th century churches of interest. It is the closest point from which one can view the ghost town of **Varosha** (Turkish: Marash). In Dherinia, turn right at an old sign that still points the way to Famagusta. Further along, the road ends abruptly at a checkpoint. A flat-roofed café-restaurant and other establishments advertise views in which the high-rise skyline of Varosha is clearly visible. It is hard to imagine that the giant tourist resort has been deserted since 1974, when 45,000 Greek Cypriots were forced to leave their town by the Turkish army. The town's inhabitants fled to the nearby British base at Dhekelia.

🛈 **Cyprus Tourism Organisation**, at the airport, tel. 643000 (open 24 hours), also in the town center, Vasileos Pavlou Square, tel. 654322.

🛏 ⑤⑤⑤ **Golden Bay**, on the Larnaka-Dhekelia road, tel. 645444, fax 645451. **Sandy Beach**, also on the Larnaka-Dhekelia road, tel. 646333, fax 646900. **Sun Hall**, Athens Ave., tel. 653341, fax 652717. ⑤⑤ **Flamingo Beach**, MacKenzie Beach, Piale Pasha St., tel. 650621, fax 656732. **Four Lanterns Hotel**, Athens Ave. 19, tel. 652011, fax 626012. ⑤ **121 Cactus**, Shakespeare St. 6-8, tel. 627400, fax 626966. **Pavion**, Faneromeni St. 11, Ag. Lazaros Sq., tel. 656688, fax 658165. HOTELAPARTMENTS: **Acropolis**, corner of Gr. Afxentiou Ave./Ermou St., tel. 623700, fax 620319. **Pasithea**, by the Salt Lake, Michael Angelo St. 4, tel. 658264, fax 625848. YOUTH HOSTELS: Nikolaou Rossou St. 27, near the Ayios Lazaros Church, tel. 621188, open all year round.

✗ Most restaurants are located beside the sea or on the road to Dhekelia. EXPENSIVE: **Al Halili**, by the Salt Lake, near the mosque of Hala Sultan Tekke. **La Gourmandise**, on the Larnaka-Dhekelia road, tel. 624100, French cuisine. MODERATE: **Marina Pub** aund **Restaurant**, on the marina, tel. 627104. **Psarolimano**, Piale Pasa 118, tel. 655408, Fish restaurant by the sea. **Scala Taverna**, Artemidos Ave., Taverna. BUDGET: **Megalos Pefkas**, at the southern end of the harbor, Greek cuisine. **Astrapi**, St. Lazarus Square, tel. 625088. **Cyprus Sky**, 1st April St., serves delicious gyros in pita bread.

🍸 DISCOTHEQUES: mostly along the Larnaca-Dhekelia road. ROCK CAFÉS: in Watkins Street and the bordering Laiki Yitonia.
A good taverna with live Greek music (from 9:30 pm) is the **Black Turtle Tavern** at the Ayios Lazaros Church, Mehmet Ali St. 11, tel. 627872.

🏛 Unless otherwise stated, the summer period is from June to September; the winter period from October to May.
Archaeological District Museum and **Kition Archaeological Site,** open in summer Mon-Fri 9 am-2:30 pm, and in winter Mon-Fri from 9 am-1:30 pm, Sat until 1 pm. **Larnaca Fort (and Museum)**, at the southern end of Athens St., in summer Mon-Fri 9 am to 7:30 pm, in winter Mon-Fri 9 am-2 pm, Sat until 1 pm. **Hala Sultan Tekke**, Mosque, daily in the summer 7:30 am-7:30 pm, in winter daily until sundown. **Municipal Art Gallery**, Europe Sq., in summer Tue-Fri 10 am-1 pm and 5-7 pm, Sat 10 am-1 pm, in winter Tue-Fri 10 am-1 pm and 4-6 pm, Sat/Sun from 10 am to 1 pm. **Pierides Collection,** Zenon Kitieus St. 4,

Mon-Sat 9 am-1 pm. **Museum of Paleontology**, Europe Sq., Tue-Fri 10 am-1pm and 4-6 pm, Sat/Sun 10 am-1 pm. **Khirokitia Excavation Site**, daily 9 am-5 pm, June-Aug until 7:30 pm. **Folk Art Museum of Lefkara**, Mon-Thurs 9:30 am-4 pm, Fri/Sat 10 am-4 pm.

📅 6. January: *Epiphany,* on this day a priest throws a cross into the sea, and the young men of the town dive in and try to be the first to retrieve it. The Carneval or *Apokreos* is a variable holiday, usually in February, with festivities, parades and masqued balls leading up to the Lenten period. In Paralimni, there is a squash competition. **Second to Last Saturday before Easter:** *Saint's Day of Lazarus*, Procession of St. Lazarus' icon in Larnaca. **May / June:** *Kataklysmos*, coinciding with Pentecost, includes games, boat races, swimming competitions, song contests and folk dancing. One day is set aside for the sole purpose of throwing water at anyone nearby, resulting in good-spirited free-for-all. **July:** *Larnaca Festival* in the court of Larnaca Fort, includes concerts, theater and dance performances as well as art exhibitions. **Mid-September:** Week-long open-air Film Festival in Larnaca Fort.

➕ Emergencies: for police, fire or medical emergencies dial 199. **Hospital:** New Hospital, Mystras St., tel. 630312. **Police:** Arch. Makarios III Ave., tel. 630200.

✉ Post Office: King Paul Sq., next to the Tourist Office, tel. 630180, open in summer Mon-Fri 7:30 am-2 pm and 4-6 pm, Sat 9 am-11 am, closed Thursday afternoons. Off-season daily from 7:30 am-2 pm and 3:30-5:30 pm, Thursdays until 6 pm, Saturdays 9-11 am.

🚌 BUSES: All buses to **Ayia Napa** and **Paralimni** (tel. 21321) and to **Nikosia** and **Limassol** (tel. 654890) depart from the bus stop opposite the Four Lanterns Hotel on the Phinikoudes shore promenade. The No.19 city bus makes trips every hour to the airport weekdays from 6 am to 6 pm, departing from Ayios Lazaros Church. *CAR RENTAL:* **Astra** 3, Leoforos Artemidos Ave. 3, tel. 624422. **Hertz**, in the International Airport, tel. 643388. **Petsas**, Karydes Court, Grig. Afxentiou Ave., tel. 623033, and also at Larnaca Airport, tel. 643350. *SERVICE (GROUP) TAXIS:* **Makris**, King Paul St. 13, tel. 652929. **Acropolis Vassos**, opposite the Tourist Office, tel. 655555. **Kyriakos**, Hermes St. 20, tel. 655100. *TAXIS:* 24-hour service for the following companies: **Akropolis**, Gladstone St., Acropolis Sq., tel. 652531. **Pentafkas**, M. Nikolaides St. 2, tel. 656984. **Omonia**, Pierides St. 24, tel. 652800.

🛍 Cypriot Arts and Crafts are available for sale in the small Cyprus Handicraft Service Shop, on Kosma Lyssioti Street. Hem-stitch embroidery and silver filigree work can be found in Lefkara. **Hand-painted icons** are for sale in the monasteries of Ayia Varvara and Ayios Minas.

ℹ Cyprus Tourism Organization in Ayia Napa, Leoforos Kryou Nerou 12, tel. 721796.

✉ 😊😊😊 Vrissiana Beach, Protaras, tel. 831216, fax 831221. **Nissi Beach**, Ayia Napa, tel. 721021, fax 721623. **😊😊 Nissi Park**, Ayia Napa, tel. 721121, fax 722196. **Pernera Beach Hotel**, Pernera Beach, tel. 831011, fax 831020. **😊 Pambos Magic**, Ayia Napa, tel. 721214. **San Antonio**, on the Paralimni-Protaras road, tel. 821561, fax 826097. *HOTEL APARTMENTS:* **Farkonia**, Pernera, tel. 831180, fax 831812. **Happy Days**, on the road to Protaras, tel. 831010, fax 820756. *YOUTH HOSTEL:* Dionysios Solomos St. 23, tel. 723113.

🏕 Ayia Napa Camping, tel. 721946, west of Ayia Napa. There is room for 150 tents/caravans, only a few meters from the beach.

🍴 Mersinia, on the outskirts of Ayia Napa, on the road to Paralimni, tel. 722640, both Greek and continental cuisine. **Kanati**, Makarios 17, in the center of Paralimni, café-restaurant with shady arbor. **Patio Mazery**, Ayia Napa, on the village square, tel. 721094, steaks and traditional Greek cuisine. **Taylors**, Dherinia (4 km north of Paralimni), excellent food, reasonable prices. **Famagusta Beach View Restaurant**, Dherinia, best view of the ghost town of Varosha from here.

📅 Weekends from March through November: *Ayia Napa Festivities*, concerts and traditional dancing in the Ayia Napa monastery. **May:** *Anthesia* Flower Festival with folkloric show and floral parade, in the stadium of Paralimni. **Early August:** Week-long folkloric *Paralimni Festival.*

🏛 Ayia Napa Monastery and **Makronissos Rock Tombs,** open daily from sunrise to sunset. **Malacology Museum** in the Town Hall, Ayia Mavra St., Mon-Sat 9 am-2 pm, Mon and Thur also 4-6:30 pm (Oct-Apr 3-5:30 pm).

✉ Post Office: Ayia Napa, Dionysou Solomou St. 8, tel. 721550, Mon-Fri 7:30 am-2 pm, also Thursdays 3:30-6 pm.

🚌 BUSES: **Paralimni Bus**, tel. 821318, Route: Paralimni Church–Protaras Hotel District–Larnaca, Mon-Sat 6:30 am-4 pm (7 trips), in summer until 5:30 pm; Route: Paralimni Church–Nikosia, Mon-Sat 7 am; Route: Paralimni Church–Protaras Hotel District–Ayia Napa, in summer hourly from 7 am on. *CAR, MOTORCYCLE AND BICYCLE RENTAL:* **Petsas**, Ayia Napa, Leoforos Nissi Ave. 20, tel. 721774. **Happiness Tours & Rentals**, Tefkrou Anthia 20, tel. 722580. *TAXIS:* **Makronissos**, tel. 721777. **Eman**, Loukas St. 1A, tel. 721379. **Paralimni**, tel. 823110.

THE LEGACY OF THE CRUSADERS

**LIMASSOL
LIMASSOL DISTRICT
KOURION
PITSILIA
NATURE WALKS**

Limassol

LIMASSOL

Limassol is a district encompassing the entire spectrum of Cypriot life. **Limassol** ❶ itself is a lively modern city, dubbed "The Little Paris of Cyprus" by local boosters because of its energy, nightlife and joie de vivre. Much of this is centered around wine making and the enjoyment of its output, since Limassol is the center of the major wineries in Cyprus. But quite unlike Paris, Limassol has not protected its architectural and cultural heritage. In the last two decades it has instead concentrated its energies on constructing modern buildings, mainly catering to tourism and trade with the Middle East.

Much of the economic growth in Limassol has occurred because of mercantile development. Because of a liberal tax structure, favorable climate and highly-qualified work force, Cyprus has rapidly expanded as an offshore center for financial trading, and for shipping companies doing business outside their own domestic market. Cyprus has the fastest growing shipping register in the world, numbering 2,500 at present, and many of the offices of these lines are in Limassol.

Left: Coffee house in the Turkish quarter of Limassol.

The population of greater Limassol is about 175,000. It has doubled since the division of the island in 1974, when refugees streamed in from the northern part of the island, making Limassol today the second largest city in Cyprus.

Limassol did not become important until the Middle Ages, when Amathus fell. The Latin form of it's name derives from the Greek *Lemesós*, which is itself said to have developed from the word *nemesos* ("in-between"), referring to the ancient city's position between Amathus to the east and Kourion to the west.

Richard the Lionheart of England landed here on his way to Jerusalem during the Third Crusade in 1191. In another ship was his betrothed, Berengaria of Navarra, accompanied by his sister Joanna, Queen Dowager of Sicily. According to legend, they were shipwrecked at Amathus. The tyrannical Isaac Comnenos wanted to capture both of them, but King Richard came to their rescue at the last minute. He was so infuriated at Comnenos' treatment of his fiancée and sister that he went into battle against him. Comnenos was eventually defeated, and Richard and Berengaria were married on May 12, 1191, probably in the chapel of the castle of Limassol. Immediately afterwards, Richard had Berengaria crowned Queen.

Above: Examples of Cypriot folk art in the Museum of Limassol.

Although a great deal of Limassol's history is associated with the crusaders, none of them came to Cyprus to conquer the island. After the fall of Acre in 1291, Limassol passed into the guardianship of the Knights Templar. But the wealth and power of the Knights gave rise to envy and distrust. Philippe IV of France finally declared them heretics, and by1312 the order was disbanded. The property of the Templars was handed over to the Knights of St. John of Jerusalem. They then built the fortress at Kolossi, west of Limassol, where they proceeded with the successful cultivation of wine and sugar cane. But Limassol suffered from consistent damage over many centuries, by numerous earthquakes and raids by Genoese, North Africans and Turkish invaders. Limassol's fortunes did not begin to rise again until the 1880s under the rule of the British, assisted by economic developments such as the building of a new pier.

The Old Town of Limassol

The best place to start a visit to the Old Town is the **Castle ❶**, on a side street off Irinis Street. The present building dates from the 14th century, although part of the west wall originated in an earlier Byzantine fortification in which Richard the Lionheart and Berengaria might have been married. The castle includes a very interesting and well laid out **Medieval Museum**. On the side streets surrounding the museum are iron and copper workshops. Streets such as Ankara, Evkaf and Safi are reminders of the former Turkish-Cypriot inhabitants who lived in this district, many of whom relocated to Kyrenia after the division of the island. To the northeast of the castle is the **Djami Kebir Mosque ❷**, and at the end of Ankara Street is another mosque overlooking the **Turkish Cemetery** next to the usually dry Garyllis River. The entrance to the cemetery is walled in.

Ayia Napa Church ❸, dating from 1903, is the massive stone building east of

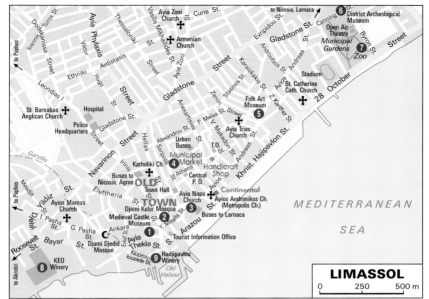

LIMASSOL

0   250   500 m

Limassol

the mosque on Ayios Andreas – or Saint Andrew – Street.

Interspersed between the produce stalls inside the cavernous old hall of the **Market ④**, behind the central post office north of Athens Street, are makeshift shops selling baskets, weavings and other local handicrafts. In the back courtyard are shops with a large selection of cheeses, sausages and natural yoghurt.

The **Folk Art Museum ⑤** has a delightful collection of tradtional costumes, farm and household tools, and examples of local handicrafts including *sandoukia* or carved wooden dowry chests, and *anathrika*, which are sturdy footstools made with reeds.

The **District Museum ⑥** on Byron Street across from the **Curium Palace Hotel** has a good collection of findings from, amongst other places, the ancient towns of Kourion and Amathus.

The nearby **Municipal Gardens** contain a small **zoo ⑦**, where a pair of mouflons can be seen. In the wild they live west of the Troodos Mountains, but are extremely shy creatures and catching a glimpse of one is a rare event indeed.

Limassol's annual two-week wine festival in September is an excellent excuse for exuberant celebration accompanied by local wine, Cypriot specialties and lively folkloric performances. Wine enthusiasts should visit the **KEO Winery ⑧** south of Franklin Roosevelt Street (Paphos Road), which gives tours of its winery and brewery every weekday morning, as does the **Hadjipavlou Winery ⑨**, at the Old Port, noted for its brandy. Both allow time for a sampling of the products at the end of the tour.

West of the industrial quarter is the new port of Limassol, constructed after 1974, where today nearly all the freight and ferry traffic to Cyprus is handled.

LIMASSOL DISTRICT

Amathus and Kolossi

Many of Limassol's most beautiful beaches belong to the hotels located east of the town, around Potamos Yermasoyias and near the archaeological site of Amathus. The beaches of the **Amathous Beach**, **Le Meridien** and other hotels are accessible to non-residents for a small fee.

Dassoudi Beach ❷, belonging to the Cypriot Tourist Association (CTO), is situated east of town and is very well laid-out, with tennis and volleyball courts, and playgrounds. Large expanses of the grounds are pleasantly shaded by pines and the water is very clean. **Lady's Mile Beach ❹**, south of **Akrotiri Bay**, is a long stretch of sand close to the British military base. It is named after the favourite horse of a British officer who used to ride here regularly.

The city of **Amathus ❸** is about 11 kilometers east of Limassol, directly behind the **Limonia Bay Hotel**. Along the shore are the protruding walls of the ancient lower city, submerged in the water.

A visit to Limassol's District Museum to see the Oriental-influenced statues of Egyptian deities and ornate capitals will convey the exotic flavor of the original settlement, and is recommended before visiting the site itself. Excavations continue on what was one of nine original city kingdoms of Cyprus and promise to yield many more significant finds.

Amathus was originally settled in the 11th century B.C. and it prospered through trade with both the Greeks and the Levantines. It remained independent, and was never taken over by the Greeks. Yet it was never conquered by the Hellenes and was one of the most powerful states of the Cypro-Geometric Period. In the revolt of 499/498 B.C., Amathus went against all the other Cypriot kingdoms and sided with the Persians. Capital of one of the four districts of the island under the Romans, Amathus began to decline in Byzantine times. Richard the Lionheart is believed to have landed here in 1191, shortly before marrying Berengaria.

Excavations brought to light the remains of a sidewall of shops, a circular building, and an early Byzantine workshop. The circular building was a *valaneion*, or public bath house, similar to those at Kition in the Larnaca District.

The major portion of the site lies up the hill to the north of the main road before the Amathus Beach Hotel, which has a **7th century B.C. tomb** on display, just next to the tennis courts. The first discoveries of this site were houses of the Hellenic Period still inhabited in the first century A.D. The paved **lower city** has been the source of capitals, columns and entablatures.

A dirt track encircles the **Akrotiri Peninsula**, leading past the **Monastery of St. Nicholas of the Cats ❺**. This monastery was founded in the year 325 by a group of monks sent to Cyprus by Emperor Constantine. Its name is derived from the cats that were brought here, supposedly by Constantine's mother, St. Helena of the Cross, to control the snake population. The stone building standing here today, built between the 13th and 15th centuries, was abandoned shortly after Turkish rule began in 1570.

The road from the monastery continues past the cliffs of **Cape Gata ❻** (*gata* is "cat" in Greek), and continues around the **Salt Lake**, a resting place for migrating birds.

★Kolossi Castle ❼, about 9 kilometers west of Limassol and once the seat of the garrison headquarters of a small group of Knights of St. John of Jerusalem, is one of the most beautiful buildings dating from the Lusignan era. Following the fall of the last crusaders' fortress in the Holy Land, the order found temporary sanctuary on the island of Cyprus, before they relocated to the Greek island of Rhodes in 1309. To guarantee their ruling power, the Lusignans presented them with land and 60 villages in the Limassol District, the villagers of which had to cultivate sugar cane and vineyards for the

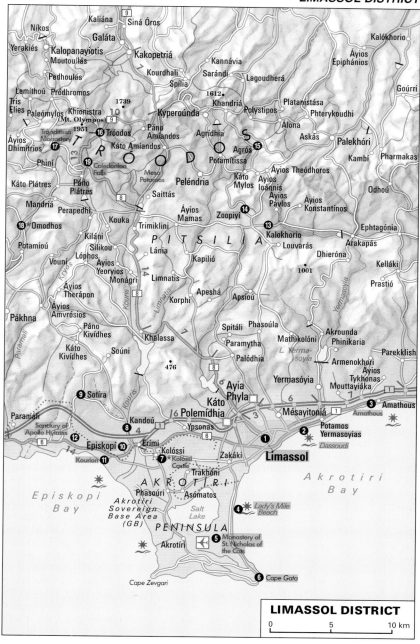

LIMASSOL DISTRICT

0   5   10 km

Knights. The sugar cane was refined in a hall beside the castle, which still exists today. The wine was exported by the Knights to Rhodes and other places under the name of *Commandaria*. This wine is still produced today by a number of vineyards in Cyprus, and is enjoyed both as an aperitif and a dessert wine.

The present **keep** was rebuilt by the Knights in 1454, on the remains of an earlier structure, and resembles a typical Gothic fairy-tale castle, with 3 meter thick walls and a drawbridge. In the garden is an aqueduct supplying cool water from the hills, which once powered a mill in which sugar cane was pressed.

Sotira and Episkopi

Just past Erimi, a road to the right leads to **Kandou ❽**, which since 1974 has been occupied by refugees from the north. A sign shows the way northwestwards to the village of **Sotira ❾**, which is made up of picturesque stone houses. The archeological site of the **Teppes** Neolithic settlement, situated on a 322 meter high hill, offers a splendid view of the surrounding Troodos Mountains and the sea. Its strategically advantageous position, combined with an abundant water supply from two springs, attracted ancient settlers. Foundations of the single-roomed sub-rectangular and oval habitations of the Aceramic Neolithic period indicate that they had flat roofs, circular platform hearths and benches.

Sotira's history, along with that of the other settlements on the southern side of the island, was abruptly terminated around 3800 B.C., probably by a series of earthquakes. The oldest pottery, painted combed ware with surprisingly elaborate wavy banded decoration, tools of chipped stone, and bone implements which were found here, can today be seen on display

Right: Sunset in the Roman Theater of Kourion.

in the Nicosia and Limassol District Museums.

The site of **Kaminoudhia** (meaning "kilns"), just 250 meters north of Sotira, dates back to the transitional Chalcolithic to Early Bronze Period. In some ways it represents a radical break with the earlier Chalcolithic Period, primarily notable for remains of a number of large multi-roomed houses; small rock-cut burial chambers containing pots and copper weapons and stone and shell ornaments, and entered by a *dromos* (entranceway). Comparisons between the pottery and metal types of Anatolia and those of Cyprus indicate that an immigration from the northern mainland must have occurred.

Findings from the entire area are displayed in the **Kourion Museum** of **Episkopi ❿**.

KOURION

Kourion ⓫ (Latin: *Curium*) was presumably founded near the Temple of Apollo in the 16th century B.C. by Dorians from Argos in Greece. Herodotus mentions that it was their home around 1200 B.C. The name Kourion possibly comes from Koureus, who was the son of a Greek immigrant. It has been made evident from a tribute list of Sargon II that the Kourion dynasty was dominated by Assyrians around 700 B.C.

In the 499/98 B.C. revolt against the Persians, Kourion initially sided with Athens, but defected at the last minute, providing Persia with the extra cover it required to take control of the entire island. In the attack on Persia at the Siege of Tyre in 332 B.C., Pasicrates, Kourion's last king, once again switched loyalties and supported Alexander the Great by leading his fleet. Kourion flourished and prospered under Roman rule. Like so many other coastal cities, it was besieged by Arab raids during the mid-seventh century. It sank into complete insignifi-

Limassol

cance when its population moved inland to Episkopi.

Getting Around

The excavation grounds of Kourion can be accessed by car. The paved road leading here ends at a parking lot beside the **Eustolios Complex**, a palatial private building that was probably later converted into a public recreation area. It houses a Roman bath complex with thermal springs constructed in the fifth century A.D.

The visitor is greeted by the following words, sunk into the mosaic in the vestibule: "Enter and bring good luck to this house." In the central room of the bathhouse there is an outstanding mosaic with four scenes, of which the panel featuring birds and fish is especially beautiful. The most famous mosaic is that of *Ktisis*, the founding spirit, depicted as a pensive woman holding a measuring rod almost exactly the length of one Roman foot.

The neighbouring **Theater**, built from huge limestone blocks in Hellenistic style in the late second century B.C., is used today for the annual summer Shakespeare Festival and other productions. Its orchestra was circular, and classical tragedies of Euripides and Sophocles, along with Aristophanes' comedies, were performed on a small raised stage. Audiences sat in the fan-shaped auditorium and enjoyed the colorful performances of the masked actors and chorus.

In Roman times (1st/2nd centuries A.D.), the chorus lost its significance and the orchestra was reduced to a semicircle. The wings of the auditorium were shortened and seats reduced to 3,500. The structure was walled in, cutting the audience off from the sea view. An new stage and scenery building were then added.

In the third century A.D., the structure was rearranged for the spectacle of hunters pursuing wild animals. Natural caves underneath the theater were probably used to keep the unfortunate beasts.

Not far from the entrance to the entire site, a broad path brings you to a fence which secures an excavation site in which archaeologists still work, but closed to the public. They have so far uncovered, among other things, a so-called **Nymphaeum**, a well house dedicated to water spirits. The ruins of the early Christian **Basilica** (5th century), on the other hand, is open to visitors. The transition to Christianity on this island, once so firmly entrenched in paganism, was gradual. It seems the way was paved, quite literally, by earthquakes in the fourth century, for the erection of Christian buildings among the pagan ruins. Acanthus capitals from Roman buildings graced four columns supporting a timber and tile superstructure over the altar.

From the Basilica a narrow path along the edge of the excavation site leads to the

Above: Perfect proportions in the Temple of Apollo Hylates. Right: Behind the walls of Trooditissa Monastery - a view reserved by the monks for only orthodox Christians.

House of Gladiators, from the fourth century A.D. The floor mosaic here depicts gladiators, who might have fought their actual battles in the Theater. In the center you can see *Margareitis* and *Ellinikos* with their swords drawn, and next to it are two further gladiators, one named *Lytras*, who is being separated from his opponent by a certain *Dareios*, who was probably a Persian referee.

On the path from the excavation site to the beach of Kourion is the little **Chapel of Ayios Hermoyenis**, which is set in a eucalyptus grove. Hermoyenis was a so-called new martyr - a Turkish Moslem who had converted to Christianity, which is the reason he was martyred. Beside the chapel is the eponymous restaurant which is a good place to take a midday break. Opposite from here, a large Mycenaean grave was discovered only 10 years ago, which can now be viewed underneath its modern new protective roof.

The Stadium and Temple of Apollo

The U-shaped **Stadium**, two kilometers west of Kourion and just north of the Paphos road, was constructed in the second century A.D. especially for competitive racing. Its name derives from the distance covered - approximately 186 meters, called a *stadium*. Athletes formed guilds honoring Herakles as their patron saint and toured throughout the entire Roman Empire in order to compete. Only a few of the original seven rows of stone seats, accommodating 6,500 people, remain.

The eighth century **Temple of Apollo Hylates ⑫** lies one kilometer west of the stadium. Apollo was worshiped here under the epithet *Hylates* or "Protector of the Woodland." Revealing vignettes are provided from the terra cotta votive offerings of the seventh and sixth centuries B.C., found in the semicircular votive pit south of the Temple. Especially charming are the figures circling a tree whilst doing

a ritual dance. The dancers partly wear bull's head masks, attesting to the continuing importance of the bull cult in pagan worship. Chariot groups and sometimes armed horsemen, did not make their appearance later.

PITSILIA

The foothill region of the Troodos Mountains, known as **Pitsilia**, is a wonderfully refreshing area of unspoiled villages taking pride in both their traditional architecture and equally renowned hospitality. Houses are often made of uncut hard stone called *sieropetres*, the spaces filled in with smaller stones and gravel, accenting the attractive textures and colors. The roofs of the hill dwellings covered in red tiles, giving them a wonderfully rustic aspect when viewed from afar.

Heading north from the east side of Limassol, you come to the interesting town of **Kalokhorio** ⑬, with its striking **Church of Ayios Yeoryios**, a rustic gem containing interesting murals which are worth viewing. **Zoopiyi** ⑭ farther north is noted for its mellow, nutty-flavored *Commandaria* dessert wine, which can be sampled and purchased in local shops. **Agros** ⑮, situated more than 1,000 meters above sea level and laid out in a semi-circle over terraces, is the main village of Pitsilia and the location of the best hotel in the region, the **Rodon**. Roses grow in the area, and their petals are distilled into rose water in the springtime. Agros is also known for its meat products: *loundsa*, a type of smoked pork, *chiromeri*, air-cured ham, and *loukanika*, richly-spiced sausages. In the **village church** of **Panayia Eleoussa** (19th century), there is an icon of the Virgin Mary, said to have been painted by Luke the evangelist.

Troodos ⑯, at an altitude of 1,725 meters above sea level, is the highest inhabited area in Cyprus and is popular for winter sports and as a summer destination for, among other things, hiking, for which there are numerous trails. From Troodos a road winds, with many hairpin bends on the way, through spectacular scenery with huge pine and aspen trees, and leads to the **Trooditissa Monastery** ⓱. The central church was built in 1731 on the base of an earlier building from the mid-13th century. Its stable-like interior with walnut carvings give it a very rustic look. The miracle-working *Icon of the Virgin Mary* is gilded in gold and silver. But the monastery only allows visits by Orthodox Christians; tourists are not welcome.

★**Omodhos** ⓲, a few kilometers further southwest, is set among vineyards. The church of the **Holy Cross Monastery** contains a piece of the True Cross and ropes that bound the hands of Christ. Omodhos is famous for its beautiful lace. Samples of it can be purchased at the fair that takes place near the monastery each year on September 14.

NATURE WALKS

The most interesting walks in the Limassol District can be made starting from Troodos, at least in summer, when the cool fresh air of the mountains can be best enjoyed.

The four-kilometer ★**Caledonia Trail**, called the "Trail of Nightingales," follows the Kryos stream. The walk is not difficult, but be sure to wear good hiking boots, as the stream has to be crossed quite often.

The walk to Platres begins 1.6 kilometers south of Troodos on the Platres Road, where a signpost reads "Caledonian Trail 500 meters" and the track begins under a wooden archway. It is a very beautiful area displaying luxurious growth of high forests and many bushes and ferns. The trail leads to the **Caledonian Falls** ⓳, the island's only notable waterfall. From here you can continue on the Caledonia Trail or via a wide forest trail to the trout farm at **Psilo Dendron**. In the restaurant here you can enjoy a delicious meal before you either take a room for the night, or else take a bus or taxi back to your hotel.

LIMASSOL (☎ 05)

🄸 **Cyprus Tourism Organisation**, Spyrou Arouzou St. 15, tel. 362756 and George St. 35, Potamos tis Germasogeias, tel. 323211.

▦ ❺❺❺ **Amathous Beach**, Amathous, 9 km east of Limassol, tel. 321152, fax 327494, elegant hotel with beautiful seaside location. **Elias Beach,** Amathous, 11 km east of Limassol, tel. 325000, fax 320880, near ancient Amathus, has a horseback riding center. **Le Meridien Limassol,** 12 km east of Limassol, tel. 634000, fax 634222, beautiful location by the sea. **Churchill Limassol**, 28th October St., Ayios Athanasios, tel. 324444, fax 323494, elegant. ❺❺ **Adonia Beach**, Amathous, 9 km east of Limassol, tel. 321111, fax 310933. **Ariadne**, 28th October St. 333, tel. 359666, fax 357421. **Curium Palace**, Byron St. 2, tel. 363121, fax 359293, elegant. **Pavemar**, 28th October St., tel. 324535, fax 324743. ❺ **Continental**, Spyros Arouzou St. 137, tel. 362530, fax 373030, friendly family-run hotel, close to Limassol Castle. **Sylva**, Grivas Dighenis St. 124, tel. 321660, fax 327121. **Trans**, Amathous, 8 km east of Limassol, tel. 322268, clean and reasonably priced. Pension **Aquarius Beach**, Amathus, 5 km east of Limassol, tel. 322042.

🄰 **Kalymnos (Governor's) Beach Camping**, tel. 63 2300, 20 km east of Limassol, open throughout the year. HOTEL APARTMENTS: **L'Onda Beach**, George St., Potamos Yermasoyias, tel. 321821, fax 320040, super-deluxe designer suites, restaurant with orchestra music, recreation: horseback riding, squash and tennis. **Azur Beach**, Potamos Yermasoyias, tel. 322667, fax 321897, lovely beach location, roomy apartments, friendly management, bar and restaurant.. **Bertha**, Amathus, 9 km east of Limassol, tel. 322324, fax 356286. **Lime Gardens**, Tinos St. 4, Potamos Yermasoyias, tel. 320033. **Old Bridge**, Kranos St. 13, Potamos Yermasoyias, tel. 321200, fax 329421, charming location in a citrus grove.

🄴 **Blue Island**, 3 Amathountos Ave., Old Limassol-Nikosia Road, tel. 321466, very popular restaurant, high quality. **Ladas**, Sadi St. 1, tel. 365760, at the Old Harbor, good *meze*, good seafood at reasonable prices. **Churchill Limassol**, 28th October St., Ayios Athanasios, tel. 324444, French cuisine. **Maharaja Indian Restaurant**, at the corner of Rigas Phereos and Grivas Dighenis Streets, tel. 376451, Indian cuisine. **Porta**, Yenethliou Mitella 17, tel. 360339, good food, live guitar music and sometimes even folk dancing. **Vassilikos**, Ayios Andreas St. 252, tel. 375972, Live Greek music Monday through Friday from 8 pm onwards.

Arkhontissa, Makarios Ave. 103, tel. 337788. **Roussos Beach Disco**, Potamos Yermasoyias, 5 km east of Limassol, tel. 322322.

Unless otherwise stated, the summer period is from June to September; the winter period from October to May.

Archaeological District Museum, Byron St., in summer Mon-Sat 9 am-5 pm, Sun 10 am-1 pm, in winter Mon-Sat 9 am-4 pm, Sun 10 am-1 pm, **Folk Art Museum**, Ayios Andreou St. 253, Mon, Wed and Fri 8:30 am-1 pm and 4-6:30 pm, Tue, Thurs and Sat 8 am-12:30 pm, in winter afternoons 3-5:30 pm. **Limassol Castle**, between Ayios Thekla and Ankara St., tel. 330419, houses the **Medieval Museum**, in summer Mon-Sat 9 am-7:30 pm, in winter until 6 pm. **Municipal Art Gallery**, tel. 343212, permanent and temporary exhibitions in summer Mon-Sat 8:30 am-1 pm, Mon-Wed and Fri also 4-6 pm, in winter Mon-Sat 8:30 am-12:30 pm. **Kolossi Castle**, 8 km west of Limassol, open daily. **Kourion**, ancient site 2 km west of Limassol on the way to Paphos, reached by service taxi from Limassol or via bus, which stops in front of Limassol Castle. **Kourion Museum**, in the George McFadden House in Episkopi, north of Kourion, Mon-Sat 8 am-2 pm, bus no. 16 to Kourion also stops in Episkopi. **Kolossi, Amathus, Kourion Castles** and the **Temple of Apollo Hylates**, are open daily in summer 9 am-7:30 pm, in winter Mon-Sat 9 am-3 pm, Sun 9am-2 pm.

Throughout the year: Classical Musical Recitals in the Dr. Nefen Michaelides School of Music. **Beginning of February:** Skiing competition on the slopes of Mount Olympos, Troodos, information from the Cyprus Ski Federation, tel. 02/36 5340, fax 02/44 8777. **8th and 9th week before Easter:** *Apokria*, street carnival beginning on the last Thursday before Lent. **May:** *Anthestiria*, flower festival, Lanition Stadium. **First two weeks of June:** Open-air festival with music, dancing, theater, sports and events with focusing on a different theme every year. **End of June:** *Shakespeare Festival* at the Kourion Theater. **July and August:** *Ancient Greek Drama Festival* in the Kourion Theater. **July 25-26:** *Ayia Paraskevi Day*, in the Ayia Paraskevi Church, Yermasoyias, 5 km northeast of Limassol. **End of August**: *Yermasoyias Festival* at the Potamos Yermasoyias hotel area, with music, dancing and theatrical performances. **Beginning of September:** Wine festival in the Municipal Gardens of Limassol.

Hospital: Limassol Hospital, tel. 330356.

Central Post Office, Arch. Kyprianou St.; afternoon services and poste restante: 1 Gladstone St., tel. 330143.

BUSES: **Bus Station,** urban buses, Andreas Themistokles St., near Anexartisias St., tel. 370592.

Kemek Station, to Nicosia and Agros, corner of Irini St./Enosis St., tel. 747532. **Kallenos,** to Larnaca from the Old Harbor, tel. 04/654850. *CAR RENTAL:* **Chris Self Drive Cars**, Arch. Makarios Ave. 178, tel. 371 891. **Europcar**, Omonoias Ave. 18-40, tel. 316789. **Petsas & Sons,** George I. St., Sea Breeze Court 1, near the Apolloni Beach Hotel, tel. 323672. *SERVICE (GROUP) TAXIS*: **Akropolis**, Spyrou Arouzou St. 49, tel. 366766. **Kyriakos/Karydas**, Thessalonikis St. 21, tel. 360261, to Nicosia and Paphos. **Makris**, Hellas St. 166, tel. 365550, to Larnaca and Paphos.

The local tailors are known for their fast, high-quality work. Leather goods, such as jackets and bags in the latest fashions, are also handmade.

PISSOURI

@@@ **Columbia Pissouri Beach**, tel. 221201, fax 221505. @ **Bunch of Grapes Inn**, tel. 221275, fax 222510. *HOTEL APARTMENTS:* **Kotzias**, tel. 221014, fax 222449.

TROODOS-REGION (☎ 05)

AGROS

@@ **Rodon**, tel. 521201, fax 521235, lovely view, pool. @ **Vlachos**, tel. 528930, cozy, family-style hotel. **Meteora**, simple taverna, large selection of typical regional dishes, including soups and stews, excellent *meze*, tel. 521331.

PLATRES

Cyprus Tourism Organisation at the main square of Pano Platres, tel. 421316, open April through October.

@@@ **Forest Park**, tel. 421751, fax 421875, 80 rooms. @@ **Edelweiss**, tel. 421335, fax 422060. **New Helvetia**, tel. 421348, fax 422148.

HOTEL APARTMENTS: **Paul's**, tel. 421425.

Psilo Dendro, large forest inn on the edge of the village beside a trout-breeding facility, only open until 4 pm, except in August.

TROODOS

@@ **Jubilee**, tel. 421647, fax 421628, in a pine forest, nature trails, close to the Sun Valley ski area. *YOUTH HOSTEL:* in the pine forest, 400 meters from Troodos Square on the Kakopetria-Troodos road, tel. 422400, open April through October.

Troodos Camping Site, tel. 421624, situated at a junction to Kakopetria, open May through October.

SKIING: T-bar lift in service at the Khionistra from late December to early February, for information: Cyprus Ski Club, Nikosia, tel. 02/365340.

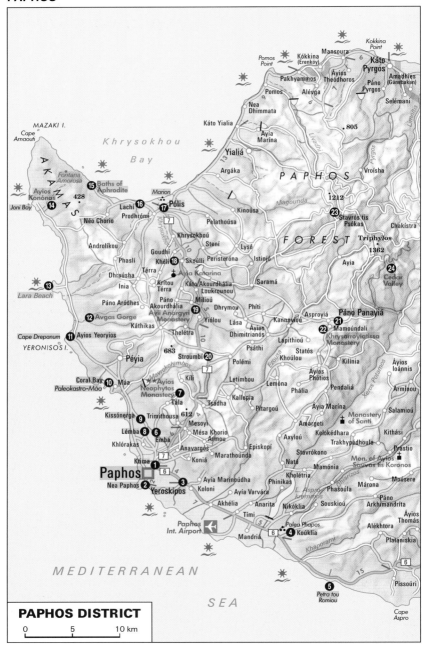

MAZAKI I.

Cape
Arnaouti

Khrysokhou

Bay

Fontana
Amorosa

15 Baths of
Aphrodite

Ayios
Konónas **14**

Joni Bay

Marion

A K A M A S

428

Néo Chorio

Lachí **16** Pólis
Prodhrómi **17**

7

Pelathoúsa

Androlíkou

Phaslí

Dhroúsha

Inia

Páno Aródhes

13

Lara Beach

Pómos
Point

Kókkina
(Erenköy)

Pakhyammos

Pómos   Alévga

Nea
Dhimmata

Káto Yialia

Ayía
Marína

Argáka

Mansoura

Áyios
Theódhoros

*Kokkina
Point*

**Káto
Pyrgos**

Páno
Pyrgos

Selémani

Amadhíes
(Günebakın)

. 805

Yialiá

P A P H O S

Vroísha

Magoúnda

Livadhi

1212

Pyrgos

Limnitis

23 Stavrós tis
Psókas

F O R E S T

Triphylos
1362

Chakístra

Khrysokhoú

Stení

Lysó

Istinjó

Goudhí **18**
Khóli   Skoúlli
Térra   Ayía Katarina
Krítou   Káto Akourdhália
Térra   Loukrounoú

Peristeróna

Saramá

Ayia

Cedar
Valley **24**

Milioú

Páno
Akourdhália

Dhrymou

Phíti

12 Avgas Gorge

Áyii Anárgyri
Monastery **19**

Yíolou

Lása

Kannaviou

Asproyiá

Páno Panayiá

21

Mamoúndali

22

*Khrysorroyiátissa
Monastery*

Cape Drepanum

11 Ayios Yeoryios

YERONISOS I.

Káthikas

Theléíra

Áyios
Dhimitrianós

Lápithiou

Khoúlou

Statós

Kilínia

Áyios
Ioánnis

Péyia

683

Stroumbí **20**

7

Psáthi

Polémi

Mavrokolymbos

Coral Bay

Paleokastro–Máa

Máa **10**

Ayios
Neophytos
Monastery

Kíli

Tála

Letímbou

Tsádha

Lemóna

Kallépia

Áyios
Phótios

Pendaliá

Armínou

Ayía Marína

Salamioú

Kissónerga

Lémba **8** **6**

9 Trimithousa

612

Mesoyí

Pitargoú

Amargeti

Monastery
of Santi

Kithási

Prastio

Khlórakas

Emba

Mésa Khorio
Armou

Anavargós

Koniá

Episkopí

Marathoúnda

Axyloú

Stávrokono

Kelokédhara

Trakhypédhoula

Mon. of Ayios
Sávvas tis Koronos

Moúsere

Paphos **1**

6

Nea Paphos **2**   **3**

Yeroskípos

Ktíma   4
7

Koloni

Ayía Marinoúdha

Ayía Varvára

Natá

Mamónia

Phínikas

Akhélia

Anarita

Tími

Nikóklia

Mandriá

*L. Aspro
kremmós*

Souskioú

Phasoúla

Márona

Sarizanos

Páno
Arkhimandríta

Áyios
Thomás

Alékhtora

*Paphos
Int. Airport*

Palea Phapos **4**

Koúklia

5

6

Platanískia

6

Pissoúri

M E D I T E R R A N E A N

5

*Petra tou
Romioú*

Khaporami

15

Cape
Aspro

S E A

PAPHOS DISTRICT

0   5   10 km

APHRODITE'S HOME

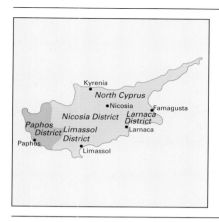

PAPHOS
YEROSKIPOS AND KOUKLIA
AYIOS NEOPHYTOS
CAPE DREPANUM
AKAMAS PENINSULA
PAPHOS FOREST

Paphos

PAPHOS

Of all the districts in Cyprus, Paphos is the richest in historical sites, legends and traditions. Long stretches of stunning sandy beaches curve lazily past deserted bays of clear turquoise water. Many legends are connected with Aphrodite, the Goddess of Love, who is said to have risen from the sea along this coast. The city of Palea Paphos was already characterized as Aphrodite's residence in Homeric times, when sensual rituals were incorporated into her worship.

Palea Paphos (Old Paphos), known today as Kouklia, is 16 kilometers from Nea Paphos and was the original center of the District in antiquity. It remained the center of worship for the cult of Aphrodite after the population was shifted to Nea Paphos in 310 B.C.

Paphos is the general name now given to the large settlement divided into the twin cities of Pano Paphos (Upper Paphos) and Nea Paphos. Ktima, as locals call Pano Paphos, stands on a hill about 1.5 kilometers from the harbor, and is an administrative center. Nea Paphos (New Paphos) is the Roman city, also called Kato Paphos (Lower Paphos), on the harbor. It contains most of the major historical sites, luxury hotels and upmarket restaurants, and is the hub of nightlife.

Ktima (Pano Paphos)

Ktima ❶, is the capital of the district. Frequent buses make the trip uphill from Nea Paphos, but if you are coming here by car it is recommended that you park in one of the town's five public parking lots and walk to the sights. Ktima (quite unlike Nea Paphos) benefits from a properly-developed town plan - here the tasteful new constructions suit the older neoclassical buildings. The **Town Hall ❶**, for example, has some lovely landscaped gardens.

Ktima was more than likely inhabited since the beginning of the Arab pirate raids on Nea Paphos, in A.D. 647. For safety, townspeople moved to their country estates, called *ktima* in Greek, on higher ground less visible from the sea but affording them a bird's eye view of invading boats.

Few of the buildings in Ktima are especially old. The oldest one of all is probably the **Djami Kebir Mosque ❷** at the northwest end of the town, which was built in 1584 over the foundations of an earlier Christian church.

The ★**District Museum ❸** contains an eclectic and ever-expanding collection of archeological artifacts from the Neolithic Period to the Renaissance. The most amusing display perhaps is a set of Ro-

Above: Nowadays the mighty Fortress of Paphos only overlooks peaceful vessels.

man clay hot water bottles, which were molded to fit the shape of the body part to be heated.

The smaller **Byzantine Museum** ❹ is housed in a section of the Bishop's Palace. Especially notable artworks here date from the 15th to the 17th centuries and include a *Virgin and Child,* portraits of the apostles, a *Birth of John the Baptist* from Kedheres, paintings of the Ascension and several nativity scenes.

Just a few steps from the Byzantine Museum is the fascinating **Ethnographic Museum** ❺ on Exo Vyrsis Street. It was lovingly gathered together piece by piece over the last 50 years, which provides a glimpse into the rural households of many years ago.

Nea Paphos

If you follow Apostolos Pavlos Avenue down the hill, it leads to the harbor of **Nea Paphos** ❷, a sleepy town until 1974, but after the division of the island the tourism boom hit hard here and was facilitated by the 1983 opening of Paphos' own international airport.

Nea Paphos was founded around 310 B.C. by Nicocles, the last ruler of the Kingdom of Paphos. The influx of pilgrims to the shrine of Aphrodite in Palea Paphos made it clear that a new settlement with a larger harbor would be required. Under the Ptolemies, Nea Paphos became the capital of the island, replacing Salamis. It was a natural choice for the seat of the government and as the shipbuilding center of the island, with lumber being supplied by nearby forests. In Roman times the town flourished and experienced a long period of peace. It is from this Roman Period that the remains of most of the main monuments date back to, except for the Tombs of the Kings. But Nea Paphos was repeatedly damaged by earthquakes, and after the seismic catastrophe of A.D 342, Salamis - now known as *Constantia* - was chosen once again as

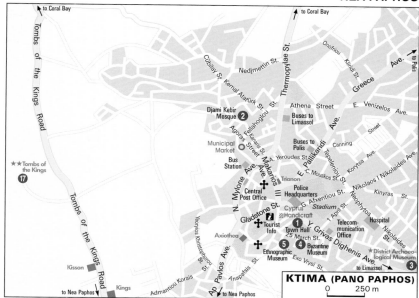

KTIMA (PANO PAPHOS)

the capital. The fate of Nea Paphos was sealed and the town fell into decline.

Inhabitants began to move to Ktima, the estates located on the hill above Nea Paphos, after the Saracen pirate raids started in A.D. 647. In that year the first large-scale Arab naval operation against Cyprus too place, led by Emir Muawiya of Syria. Moslem attacks on the island continued until A.D. 911. The political situation during these years seems hazy, but the island was probably never completely controlled by the Arabs.

The important Byzantine castle on the harbor was the site of Paphos' 1191 surrender to the legendary kind and crusader Richard the Lionheart, ushering in the Lusignan Era. At the end of the 12th century the Lusignans built the castle of Saranta Kolones on the site, a well-fortified structure destroyed by an earthquake in 1222. Instead of restoring it, the Lusignans then built a far less imposing fortress, which is still on the harbor. But before the end of the Lusignan Period (1489), Nea Paphos was deserted by its inhabitants after it was almost completely destroyed by earthquakes. By 1800, the population of Nea Paphos was barely 1,000, but this had more than doubled by 1881. This growth was spurred by the greater economic prosperity caused by the dredging of the silted harbor in 1908. The population of the town has steadily increased since that time, and is now at about 24,000 and still growing.

Getting Around: One can walk to all the major archeological sites clustered in the same area on the harbor. For visitors who only have one day to cover Paphos' sights, the Tombs of the Kings, the fort on the harbor (mainly for its excellent view of the entire area) and the mosaics of Paphos are absolute musts. The first stops should be at the Houses of Dionysus, Orpheus and Aion, and the Villa of Theseus, Roman Period villas a short distance from the harbor. In them are the finest mosaics in the eastern Mediterranean, mainly with Greek mythological themes.

The entrance to the site of the Roman villas is at the end of Kyriakou Nikolaou

Street, 300 meters from the harbor. On the right is a wooden reconstruction of the **House of Dionysus** ⑥, named for its representations of pleasure-loving Dionysus, God of Wine, featured in many notable mosaics. The house, built in the late second or early third century A.D., was, with 2,000 square meters, one of the largest Roman villas. 556 square meters in 14 rooms are covered with glorious mosaics. Over 40 rooms on two levels were around a colonnaded courtyard with a rainwater fountain. Many smaller rooms on the lower level, which had an advanced underground sewage system, were used as kitchens, workshops, stores and offices. The house was located in the middle of a thriving residential area.

A wooden walkway over unexcavated mosaics leads to the once enormous **Villa of Theseus** ⑦, 150 meters to the west. It originally had more than 100

Above: A nymph from the "Triumphal Procession of Dionysos."

rooms and corridors, indicating it was once part of the palace of the Roman governor. Its name comes from the elegant circular mosaic of the battle in the Labyrinth of Crete between the celebrated Athenian hero Theseus and the Minotaur. It was made in the third century and restored after an earthquake in the fourth century A.D. Other mosaics show *Poseidon and Amphitrite* riding on the back of a sea monster, and the *First Bath of Achilles* after his birth.

To the west is the **House of Orpheus** ⑧, where a three-paneled mosaic has been discovered: *Herakles Fighting the Lion of Nemea*, an *Amazon with Her Horse*, and a wonderful scene depicting *Orpheus Playing the Lyre*, surrounded by transfixed animals.

The mosaics and inlaid work in the **House of Aion** ⑨ are considered to be the most significant late-Roman mosaic panels in Cyprus. These include the *Birth of Dionysus*, the *Contest between Dionysus and Marsyas* and the *Beauty Contest between Cassiopeia and the Nereids*

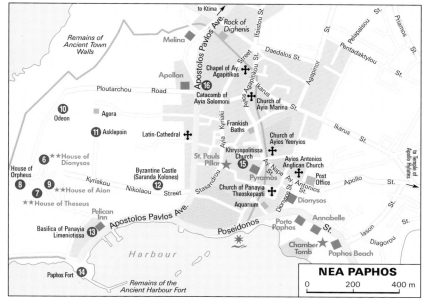

judged by Aion, the God of Eternity. Perhaps the most provocative mosaic of all and the one most often associated with Paphos on posters and picture postcards is *Leda and the Swan*, which depicts the shapely semi-clad Queen of Sparta being approached by Zeus, in love, in the form of a swan.

The artistry of these panels is of an exceptionally high standard, with rich colors and an outstanding grasp of expression. A coin finding shows that the mosaics must have been made in the second half of the fourth century, in other words at a time when Christianity had become a recognized religion, though curiously these mosaic panels still glorified pagan beliefs.

Below the modern lighthouse lie the ruins of a complex of buildings, the Odeon, Agora and Temple of Asclepius. This was probably the site of the town's acropolis, judging from Hellenistic and Greco-Roman foundation remains unearthed here. To the north of the lighthouse you can see the extensive remains

of the ancient Hellenistic town walls, a ramp and a rock bridge, which lead across a moat.

The semicircle of the **Roman Odeon** ⑩, built in the second century A.D., contains 11 restored rows of seats (originally 25), for about 1,200 spectators. From the top rows one has a clear view of the orchestra and stage, providing the perfect setting for summer performances.

Further south and below the Agora (marketplace), the **Asclepion** ⑪ once stood. The towering Roman Temple of Asclepius, the God of Medicine, was used as a medical center noted for its fasts designed to purge the system.

The ruins of the **Saranta Kolones Castle** ⑫ are visible on Kyriakou Nikolaou Street and are always accessible. The castle's name means "Forty Columns" and refers to the granite columns from previously destroyed Roman public buildings which once lay scattered over the area and which were incorporated into the building of this castle. Built by the Lusignans in the early 13th century, prob-

ably on the site of an earlier Byzantine castle, it was surrounded by a three meter thick wall once defended by eight towers of various shapes. It was largely destroyed by an earthquake in 1222.

The ruins of the Early Christian **Panayia Limeniotissa Basilica** ⓭ (Our Dear Lady of the Harbor) lie on the way to the harbor. It was severely damaged by Arabs in 653 A.D. and finally completely destroyed by an earthquake in 1153.

The most prominent building in the **harbor** is **Paphos Fort** ⓮. Originally built as a Byzantine citadel to protect the harbor, it was reconstructed by the Lusignans in the mid-13th century to replace the Saranta Kolones Castle. It was dismantled by the Venetians, who found themselves unable to defend it against the invading Ottomans, but after they occupied the island the Turks actually restored

Above: Green fee in the Secret Valley - two of the three Cypriot golf courses are in Paphos District. Right: The mysterious Tombs of the Kings, final resting place for Ptolemaic royalty.

and extended it to include a new west tower. During British occupation it was used as a salt store. It was finally declared a protected monument in 1935, but was unfortunately damaged by an earthquake in 1953. Beyond the vaulted central hall, rooms lead to the cells used when the castle was a prison, with dungeons below.

The **Church of Ayia Kyriaki**, better known as **Khrysopolitissa** ⓯, was built (as it now stands) after 1571 on the site of Roman and early Christian basilica of the fourth century. Sections of a delightful mosaic pavement, uncovered between the road and the apse, are remains of the earlier huge seven-nave basilica, the main structure of which was 53 meters long and 38 meters wide. Four pink granite columns must have supported the roof of the eastern wing. Partially covered acanthus capitals of green and white *Cipollino* marble imported from the Greek island of Evia (Euboa), as well as a few tombstones, lie on the grounds. The item attracting the most attention, however, is a rounded white marble pillar under a tree at the west gateway. According to local tradition, this is the place at which Saint Paul is said to have been bound and flogged by Romans.

Undoubtedly the most unusual monuments of Nea Paphos are the Catacombs of Ayia Solomoni and Ayios Lambrianos. They were carved into the hillside, just below the Roman city wall, in the 4th century B.C., and were later converted into chapels in the early days of Christianity. At the entrance to the underground **Catacomb of Ayia Solomoni** ⑯ is a huge pistachio tree or *pistacia atlantica*, a species from which the fairly bland *Pissa Paphitiki* gum is gathered, which is then sold in local shops. The tree looks very strange to the unitiated because it is covered with bits of cloth left by the faithful as votive offerings to Ayia Solomoni, a custom of both Christians and Moslems in the eastern Mediterranean.

The intriguing burial site known as the ****Tombs of the Kings** ⑰ (see map page 39) is about two kilometers northwest of Paphos Harbor, just off Tombs of the Kings Road heading towards Coral Bay. Despite its name, the more than 100 graves serving as the town's necropolis from the third century B.C. to the third century A.D., were the final resting place of Ptolemaic aristocracy, not of royalty.

The tombs carved into the reddish rock overhanging the sea were undoubtedly inspired by tombs in the Hellenistic necropolis of Alexandria, since no prototype for the design existed in Cyprus. A map at the entrance notes the location of the most interesting tombs, including **Tomb 5** which is very grand with its 12 elaborate Doric columns surrounding a spacious peristyle courtyard, resembling a house with atrium and peristyle. The bones found in **Tomb 7** provide evidence that both the horse and owner were buried together. **Tomb 8** was originally thought to be a royal tomb because its courtyard is decorated with a limestone falcon, the

Ptolemaic royal symbol, but it is now assumed to have held the remains of an affluent Ptolemy.

YEROSKIPOS AND KOUKLIA
(Palea Paphos)

To delve into the legend of Aphrodite, an excursion from Nea Paphos to Yeroskipos and Kouklia and finally to Petra tou Romiou must be made, where she is said to have emerged from the sea.

Yeroskipos ❸ (from the Greek *Ieros Kipos*, meaning "The Sacred Garden"), was a resting place for pilgrims on their way to the springtime celebrations at the Temple of Aphrodite and one of the silk manufacturing centers on the island, as its many mulberry trees suggest. Between 1925 and 1950 a silk factory operated here. Today its claim to fame is the manufacture of the sweet grape-flavored jelly known as *loukoumi* or Turkish Delight, created four centuries ago during the Ottoman Period. Along the main road of the town, children and their black-clad

yiayiades (grandmothers) lurk under parasols protecting them from the scorching sun, waiting for customers to buy boxes of the traditional sweets.

Most of the remaining buildings date from Byzantine times. The most outstanding Byzantine building in town is the five-domed **Church of Ayia Paraskevi**, similar to the only other one of this type left on the island in Peristerona. It was originally cruciform, but was altered by unfortunate enlargements in the 19th century and again in 1931, yet it still retains its ageless charm. The church contains some fine ninth to fifteenth century frescoes.

The 18th century **House of Hadji Smith**, now a folk museum, is situated to the east. It was the residence of Andreas Zimboulakis, named British Vice-Consul in 1799 by William Sydney Smith. To

Above: Ayia Paraskevi in Yeroskipos. Right: Casual customs - part of the cult of Aphrodite which enraged Herodot - belong to Cyprus' past; nowadays people wed in decency.

honor his benefactor, Andreas assumed the name of Hadji Smith (*Hadji* was attached to the names of Christians who had made the pilgrimage to Jerusalem).

The journey continues 10 km further on the straight route from Yeroskipos to **Kouklia** ❹ (Palea Paphos) to the **Temple of Aphrodite**. Two possible founders of the Temple of Aphrodite emerged in ancient legend. According to Pausanias' version, it was built by Agapenor, the Arcadian King of Tegea, who, while on his way home, was driven by a storm onto Cyprus' shores. The more likely founder, however, was wealthy King Kinyras, father of Adonis, who lived to a ripe old age while ruling Paphos during the time of the Trojan War. He was the first of the priest-kings, who developed religious rites adapted to the worship of Aphrodite and later Adonis. His wealth was legendary, in fact he was said to have been even wealthier than the legendary King Croesus. Kinyras' successors, called *Kynirades*, ruled until Ptolemy I replaced them with military governors in 295 B.C.

Kouklia was continuously inhabited from the 15th century B.C. until the end of the Middle Ages. In the 13th and 12th centuries B.C. Achaen Greeks (Mycenaeans) settled here. The wealth of this Late Bronze Age city must have been enormous judging from the artifacts found in the tombs of ancient cemeteries. During the Cypro-Archaic and Classical Periods (seventh to fourth centuries B.C.), Paphos reached the zenith of its influence. In the Ionian Revolt of 499 B.C., Paphos sided with the other Greek cities against the Persians, who retaliated by attacking the city in 498 B.C. In 480 B.C., Paphos contributed 12 ships to the fleet of Persian King Xerxes. Nicocles, the last king of Paphos, named Nea Paphos as the new capital around 310 B.C., overshadowing Palea Paphos. Although Palea Paphos' population shrank during the Hellenic Period and was further depleted after the serious damage caused by earth-

quakes in 15 B.C. and A.D. 323, the sanctuary of Aphrodite continued to prosper until the fourth century A.D. It was often visited by Roman emperors viewing athletic contests. Palea Paphos fell into decline in the late fourth century A.D., following Emperor Theodosius' orders that all pagan temples would be closed by decree.

Palea Paphos (Old Paphos) sits on the plateau of a limestone hill, at a distance of about 1.5 kilometers from the sea. The most notable object unearthed here was a unique cone-shaped black stone. This fertility symbol would be anointed with oil and worshiped at ancient festivals of Aphrodite. It is now on display in the Lusignan Manor Museum at the site. The worship of Aphrodite was, in its amorphous rather than human form, similar to the worship of other fertility goddesses in the Middle East.

The Paphian Temple of Aphrodite never resembled a typical Greek temple, but instead was a sanctuary similar to those found in Asia Minor and at Soli in the northern part of the Cyprus. Roman coins are the only source of depictions of the original temple. The site actually consists of two sanctuaries. The southern one was rebuilt by Romans on a Bronze Age site, and it was divided into a *temenos*, or sacred enclosure, with altars and a covered hall. The northern sanctuary was rebuilt in A.D. 77. It has a couple of halls and an east wing with an open courtyard. Like all of Aphrodite's temples it is said to be cooled by gentle breezes perfumed with flowers and herbs. A spot near the south wall of the north stoa is marked by a limestone monolith to indicate the location of the holy fertility stone. Now only wall foundations, column bases and sections of Roman mosaics remain, with more mosaics in the ruins of a house west of the north sanctuary. Some of the stone was quarried in the Middle Ages to construct a Frankish sugar refinery.

The fame of the cult of Aphrodite is based on oral tradition. In this manner, the orgiastic pagan rituals that it was connected with captured the popular imagination and attracted visitors from all over the ancient world. According to reports, the annual Aphrodite festival, with its contests and games, was the most popular in Paphos. Pilgrims wearing myrtle crowns filed in a procession, accompanied by music, along the 14 kilometer sacred path from the harbor to the temple of the Goddess of Love. On their first visit, worshippers had to give a coin to the priests, for which they received a small piece of salt, symbolic of Aphrodite's birth in the sea, and a ceramic phallus.

Prudish writers disapproved of what they labeled "religious prostitution" that was practiced in strategically-placed pleasure booths and pleasure benches in lush gardens. The historian Herodotus wrote about the custom that every young Paphian woman, rich or poor, had to serve as a priestess and sit in the temple wearing a plaited rope headband until an admirer claimed her by throwing a coin at her feet and saying, "I invoke the goddess upon you." The coins went to the temple and after the young woman had given herself to the man as a sacrifice to Aphrodite, she could go home.

"All those who were beautiful and well-built finished quickly," reported Herodotus. "But the ugly ones had to stay a long time. There are some who waited as long as three or four years." It seems that during the Roman Period the custom had degenerated and was an excuse for rampant prostitution.

Southwest of the temple is a **museum** in the former Lusignan Manor House, originally called the **Château de Covocle** and later called the *Çiftlik*, because it was the manor of a large farm (Turkish: *çiftlik*) during the Turkish Period. All that survives of the original Frankish structure is the stately Gothic hall in the east wing.

The manor is now a museum, the prize display of which is the fertility stone of

Right: Richly-colored frescoes in the monastery of Ayios Neophytos.

Aphrodite. Besides this there are objects found in the area including terra cotta figurines, weapons, jewelry, and an epigraphical collection with fragments engraved in the still undeciphered Cyprosyllabic script. From the entrance of the fort a paved path leads to a replica of the mosaic of *Leda and the Swan.* The original was recovered in London after being stolen. It is now on display in the Cyprus Museum in Nicosia.

Four kilometers southeast of Kouklia is the legendary birthplace of Aphrodite, **Petra tou Romiou** ❺, meaning "The Greek's Rock." This refers to Byzantine hero Dighenis Akritas, who is said to have flung several large rocks at the invading Saracen pirates which landed in the sea. These large boulders now mark the magnificent site at which Aphrodite is said to have emerged from the water.

**AYIOS NEOPHYTOS

Emba ❻ is at its most beautiful in the springtime, when the fields are blanketed in brilliant scarlet anemones. Notable is the **Panayia Khryseleousa Church**, whose frescoes were unfortunately ruined by an inept restorer in 1886, except for the Pantocrator on the dome. Note also the two-paneled icon dating from the 17th century, depicting the 12 apostles over the Venetian coat of arms.

The **Monastery of Ayios Neophytos** ❼ is set amidst splendid scenery on the 612 meter high Charta Summit of the Melissovouno, or otherwise known as the "Honey Mountain," which affords breathtaking vistas of Paphos and the sea below. It's easy to understand how the isolation attracted the extraordinary hermit Neophytos.,

Neophytos was born in Kato Dhrys, a small village near Kato Lefkara, in 1134. He ran off and hid in the Monastery of Ayios Khrysostomos near Buffavento rather than marry a bride chosen by his parents. When discovered, he was forced

to go home, but soon convinced his parents it was best for him to "embrace a monastic life rather than a bride." Neophytos then set off for the hills above Paphos and dug a cave with his own hands (to the left of the present 15th century monastery) where he lived from 1159 on. The problem was that his fame spread, and his quest for solitude was very much disturbed by visitors. Feeling frustrated, although already quite old, he burrowed yet another cave higher than the first one. Neophytos resided there in his final years, emerging only on Sundays to preach to his followers. Over the years Neophytos wrote a number of scholarly theology books as well as an indictment against Richard the Lionheart, calling him the "wretch."

Especially notable at the site are the well-tended gardens with olive and fruit trees, first cultivated by Neophytos, and an amazing cave, called the **Enkleistra**, in which he lived his Spartan life. A cupboard here was once filled with the skulls of his followers. A little **chapel** with a

simple wooden cross is decorated in marvelous frescoes, some dark-blue based, others brighter with rich gold accents, begun under the supervision of Neophytos by a disciple named Apseudes and continued by others after his death. The icons show influences of both the more sophisticated aristocratic Constantinople school and the softer, more popular "monastic" school. Outstanding among them are *Worship of the Three Holy Kings* and another Byzantine-style icon in which Christ, dressed in blue, is shown teaching his apostles and Neophytos, who is flanked by the archangels Michael and Gabriel.

Avoid coming here on the holy days of Neophytos, January 24 and September 28, in order to appreciate the calm beauty of the setting and evoke the spirit of the shy cleric Neophytos while listening to the church bells, monks reciting prayers, and birds chirping. At that time, religious pilgrims come in flocks to kiss the silver reliquary containing the skull of Ayios Neophytos and drink the refreshing water

from the spring near the café, said to be a disease preventative.

CAPE DREPANUM

A pleasant day trip by rental car leads from Paphos to Ayios Yeoryios and, if you leave early enough, on to the Akamas Peninsula. The first stop en route is the artists' village of **Lemba ❽**. The Cypriot artist Stass Paraskos organizes summer courses here for young painters and sculptors from around the world; a number of curious creations by the master and his pupils adorn the garden of his studio on the square. Beyond the edge of the village, a sign points the way to the "Prehistoric Village," the nearby **Lemba Experimental Village**, a chalcolithic settlement (about 3500 to 2500 B.C.). Some of the circular huts have been reconstructed and are open to the public.

Above: The grapefruit harvest at Peyia near Coral Bay. Right: One of the most beautiful bays of Cape Drepanum.

For the continuing journey you either take the coastal road or else make a short detour through the large village of **Kissonerga ❾**. It is particularly worth visiting on the Orthodox Easter Sunday, on the afternoon of which the popular "Easter Games" take place in the municipal stadium below the main street. Visitors can also join in the fun without having to register in advance. Competitions include such things as sack races and Easter egg races. The Cypriots, at least, enjoy themselves immensely at this festival.

Just past Kissongera, the coast road winds through stretches surrounded by banana plantations, before reaching **Coral Bay ❿**, a fast-expanding holiday resort apparently built without any apparent plan. It got its name for its lovely sand beaches, tinged pink by coral fragments.

On the 378 meter long, 90 meter wide and 17 meter high peninsula of **Paleokastro-Maa**, which breaks Coral Bay up into two sections, remains of a Late Bronze Age settlement were discovered,

Paphos

which was probably only inhabited from 1230 to 1200 B.C. Land and seaward walls up to four meters in thickness and the foundation walls of dwellings are all that remain today. The military settlement was probably founded by Greek and Cretan immigrants who planned to settle here temporarily and who, a generation later, became integrated into neighboring villages. A small exhibition on the excavation grounds illustrates the epoch of the Mycenaean settlement of Cyprus, relevant today vis-à-vis the current political situation. Due to the arrival of the Greeks around 1200 B.C., Cyprus became completely Grecized; which shows, as supported by archeological evidence, that Cyprus has always been a Greek island.

On the other side of the Paleokastroa-Maa peninsula lies the windsurfers paradise of **Coralina Bay.**

A road veering northwestwards through pine and juniper forests leads, after seven kilometers, to the sea at **Ayios Yeoryios** ⓫, a sparse settlement with wonderful rocky bays and sand beaches

at **Cape Drepanum**. Near the modern main church lie the fenced-in remains of an early Christian basilica. Lovely mosaics portray birds and fish. Close by is the simple Byzantine **Church of Ayios Yeoryios**, featuring two peculiarities often encountered on Cyprus: in front of the church is a tree with strips of cloth left hanging from its branches by the faithful – in this case in the hope of having a lost animal returned. The church itself has thick twine wrapped around it. Perhaps this "girding" has some connection to the girdle of Aphrodite. It is said that any man who set his eyes on it was eternally smitten by the beautiful goddess.

THE AKAMAS PENINSULA

The paved road ends in Ayios Yeoryios. From here a dusty path leads to the Akamas Peninsula. Soon a signpost points out a turnoff for the **Avgas Gorge** ⓬ (also called Avagas Gorge), which is a pleasure to hike through and for which at least two hours should be set aside.

Four kilometers farther north on the bumpy dirt road approaching the coast is **Lara Beach ⑬**. This long sandy stretch is the nesting area of the protected green and loggerhead turtles. Concerned conservationists have been patrolling the beach every summer since 1978 to protect the nests from being destroyed by tourists. Cages protect the nests from the sea turtles' natural enemies, which include crabs, foxes, crows and hawks.

About 13 kilometers further, a detour from the coastal road leads to the **Ayios Kononas Chapel ⑭**, only two kilometers inland. Here Danish archeologists have discovered the ruins of a large Greco-Roman settlement. The chapel is built above a simple Hellenic grave.

Five hundred meters after the fork leading toward the chapel, the dirt road ends at the **Bay of Joni**. From here it is best to take the already known route back to Ayios Yeorgios or else, at a signposted turnoff, take the road to the left toward **Neo Chorio**, via the east coast of the Akamas Peninsula.

Before Lachi a road forks to the north and ends at the parking lot of the **Baths of Aphrodite ⑮** (Loutra tis Aphroditis), to which a paved path leads on a two minute walk. The idyllic, shallow freshwater pool was one of Aphrodite's favorite bathing spots, where she engaged in amorous encounters with her lover Akamas. Nowadays, bathing is forbidden here. The pebble beach below the **restaurant**, however, is a great place to go for a swim, and from its terrace there is a wonderful view of the Bay of Polis. From the parking lot, a trail – not suitable for driving – leads along the north coast to the perhaps unjustly named **Fontana Amorosa**. This "Fountain of Love" is in reality nothing more than a wretched well, the water of which imparts to the drinker not eternal youth, but severe diarrhea instead.

Right: Even the very young get the best from the beach at Lachi.

Whatever you do while touring Cyprus, don't miss a visit to **Lachi ⑯** (sometimes spelled "Latsi"). This is the newest holiday resort on the island, and is most popular with younger tourists traveling individually. It has a special character thanks to its fishing harbor and the seafood restaurants along the shore promenade. Beautiful beaches stretch out on both sides of the harbor, and just about every kind of water sport can be engaged in here.

From Polis to Paphos Forest

Polis ⑦ is a pleasant seaside town and still a quiet holiday retreat, despite a dramatic increase in tourism in recent years. This is an ideal location for beach lovers who crave the simple pleasures of sand, sun and surf, but is also an important center of citrus fruit production; walnuts, almonds, carob and wheat are also harvested here in abundance. The small traditional houses of the town, with their wooden balconies and staircases, are typical examples of early 19th century Cypriot architecture.

To the northeast of Polis was the ancient copper center of **Marion**, said to have been founded in the seventh century B.C. by Athenians, and destroyed in 312 B.C. by Ptolemy (the future King Ptolemy I of Egypt). It was succeeded some decades later by a new town known as *Arsinoë*. To date a vast necropolis containing mostly Hellenic tombs has been unearthed, in which imported Attic pottery was found, with some older specimens dating from the sixth to fourth centuries B.C. Excavations here are ongoing, and it is extremely likely that new findings will be brought to light. An **archeological museum** on the main street of Polis displays objects found on sites in the region.

The Polis-Ktima road leads southwards through the Khrysokhou valley. A little to the west of the road lies **Kholi ⑱**,

Paphos

known for its 16th century **Archangel Church**, built over the base of a Venetian watchtower. Closeby is the **Ayii Anargyri Monastery** ⑲ at **Miliou**, built in 1649 in honor of the two brothers Cosmos and Damian. They were called Ayii Anargyri, or "Saints without Fees", because they gave medical treatment to the sick without any payment.

The last village before the turn-off to Paphos Forest is **Stroumbi** ⑳. The otherwise not especially attractive village celebrates an annual three day "Dionysia" wine festival in late August, at which not only local wines are sampled, but shows of Cypriot folklore can also be enjoyed.

South of Stroumbi you leave the highway and turn left onto the main road leading directly to Pano Panayia, 20 km further on.

PAPHOS FOREST

Nature lovers will be enchanted by the sites of the Khrysorroyiatissa Monastery and the Forestry Station of Stavros tis Psokas in the **Paphos Forest**. It is best go with a jeep, with a full tank of gas.

Pano Panayia ㉑ is situated about 1 km from the monastery. This is where Archbishop Makarios III was born in 1913. Here you can visit his simple birth house and see an exhibition dedicated to him in close proximity to his memorial.

Just southwest is the **Monastery of Khrysorroyiatissa** ㉒, meaning "Our Lady of the Pomegranate." It was founded by a monk named Ignatius in 1152 after he found an icon of the Virgin Mary. He was subsequently "visited" by her and was appointed the task of building a monastery to shelter it. The icon, kept in a silver-gilted case in a triangular-shaped cloister, is strangely enough the pilgrimage destination of condemned criminals, who come here to pray for mercy. Khrysorroyiatissa is surrounded by vineyards and has a widespread reputation for making the finest wine on the island, called *Monte Royia*. The monks left here years ago. During the Turkish occupation, this was known as the "Monastery of the Bell," because the abbot here had managed to circumvent the prohibition against bell ringing.

The last stage of this trip leads to **Stavros tis Psokas** ㉓, after 12 km driving on a narrow dirt road which is undriveable in poor weather. "The Cross of Measles" is so named because a spring here was reputed to cure measles (Greek: *psokas*). The expansive forest of mainly golden oak, Lebanon cedar and Aleppo pine, lends the landscape a sense of grandeur. Stavros tis Psokas has a taverna and a guest house with seven simple rooms, with a kitchen and fireplace. Rooms can be reserved for stays of up to three days. This is the realm of the indigenous moufflon, the horned sheep featured on Cypriot coins. A protected species, numbers today are estimated at only 2,000 after nearly being hunted to extinction at the turn of the century. The elusive animals are extremely shy and not easily sighted, but early birds who get up at the crack of dawn and wait quietly near a clearing may get a chance to glimpse one in the wild. Alternatively, there is a small herd in the enclosure next to the **forest rangers' station**.

For the return journey - unlike the trip coming here - take the country road in a southeasterly direction, or simply follow the signs for Kykko Monastery. After about 5 kilometers, take a right turn onto the forest road, which will lead you up to **Tripylos Peak** (1,362 m). You can park the car at the side of the road while undertaking the half-hour hike up to the peak. From the top, there is a quite magnificent view over ★**Cedar Valley** ㉔, which lies in a southerly direction, with its over 5,000 cedars and the last remaining specimens of the Troodos pine. This appears to be a practically unspoilt world unto itself! It is only on the continuing journey through the valley and further on to Pano Panayia, that you will realize that the cedars close-up are not so much upright giants as thinning windbreaks.

ℹ️ **Cyprus Tourism Organisation**, Gladstone St. 3, Ktima, tel. 232841, and at the airport, tel. 422833, opening hours coincide with flight arrivals.

🛏️ All by the sea, on Poseidonos Ave.: 😊😊😊 **Alexander the Great**, tel. 265000, fax 265100. **Annabelle**, tel. 238333, fax 245502. **Paphos Beach**, tel. 233091, fax 242818, surfboard rentals, diving school, disco. **Cypria Maris**, tel. 264111, fax 264125, situated outside town, organized entertainment available. 😊😊 **Porto Paphos**, tel. 242333, fax 241341, in town. **Paphian Bay**, tel. 264333, fax 264870, outside the town. Close to the archaeological sites, out of town: **Kissos**, Vereniki St., tel. 236111, fax 245125. **Land of the Kings**, Tombs of the Kings St., tel. 241770, fax 245594. 😊 In Nea Paphos: **Agapinor**, Nikodimos Mylonas St. 26, tel. 233927, fax 235308. **Pyramos**, Ay. Anastasia St. 4, tel. 235161, fax 242939. In Ktima: **Trianon**, Makarios Ave. 99, Tel. 232193. *YOUTH HOSTELS:* In the northeast of Ktima, Eleftherios Venizelos Ave. 37, tel. 232588, open daily 7:30-10:30 am and 4:30-11 pm, 15 minutes' walk from the town center.

🏕️ **Yeroskipou Zenon Gardens**, tel. 242277, on the beach, 3 km east of Paphos Harbor, open April through October. **Feggari Camping**, tel. 621534, Coral Bay, 11 km north of Paphos, open all year.

🍴 **Pelican**, Apostle Paul Ave., tel. 232827, seafood restaurant at the harbor. **Mediterranean Tavern**, Ay. Napa St. 3, tel. 235684, delicious fish dishes. *Meze* and *klephtiko* (lamb baked slowly in a special earthenware oven) is served at the **Demokritos Tavern**, Dionysos St. 1, tel. 233371, with music and Cypriot folk dancing. **Les Etoiles**, Diagorou St. 1, tel. 234083, international and Greek cuisine, quiet, pleasant restaurant.

📅 Unless otherwise stated, the summer period is from June to September; the winter period from October to May.

District Archaeological Museum, Grivas Dighenis Ave., tel. 240215, open in summer Mon-Sat 7:30 am-1:30 pm and 4-6 pm, Sun 10 am-1 pm, in winter Mon-Fri 7:30 am-2 pm and 3-5 pm, Sat 7:30 am-1 pm and 3-5 pm, Sun 10 am-1 pm. **Aquarium**, Artemidios St., daily 10 am-8 pm. **Byzantine Museum**, Andrea Ioannou St., Ktima, tel. 232 092, Mon-Fri 9 am-5 pm (in summer until 7 pm), Sat 9 am-2 pm. **Ethnographic Museum** (Eliades Collection), Exo Vriysis St. 1, tel. 232010, Mon-Sat 9 am-1 pm and 4-7 pm (Oct.-Apr. 3-5 pm), Sun 10 am-1 pm. **Paphos Fort**, Nea Paphos, open in summer Mon-Sat 9 am-1:30 pm, in winter Mon-Fri 9 am-2 pm, Sat 9 am-1 pm. **Royal Tombs**, tel.

240295, open in summer daily 9 am-7:30 pm, in winter daily 9 am till sunset. **Mosaics**, in the Villas of Dionysos, Theseus and Aion, Nea Paphos, tel. 240217, open in summer daily 9 am-7:30 pm, in winter daily 9 am till sunset. **Hadji Smith House** (Folk Art Museum), Yeroskipos, 3 km east of Paphos, tel. 240216, in summer daily Mon-Sat 9 am-1:30 pm, in winter daily Mon-Fri 9 am-2 pm, Sat till 1 pm. **Temple of Aphrodite** and **Paleapaphos Museum**, Kouklia, 14 km east of Paphos, in summer daily 9 am-7:30 pm, open in winter until sunset. **Paleokastro-Maa**, Coral Bay, archaeological findings Mon-Sat 10 am-4 pm. **Saranda Colones Fortress**, open to the public during the daytime.

Variable but usually in **February**: Carneval or *Apokreos*, lasts two weeks and ends on the Monday preceding Lent, with parties, fancy-dress balls and parades through the main streets of Paphos. **Monday preceding Lent**: colourful *Kite Competition* on the grounds of the castle, followed by a traditional feast. **Sunday in May**: *Anthestiria*, flower festival with a floral parade, various cultural events and exhibitions of Cypriot flora, particularly that of the Akamas Peninsula. **May or June**: Coinciding with Pentecost, the variable holiday *Kataklysmos* (Festival of the Flood) is a religious festival celebrated only in Cyprus. **June through September**: *Pafia Festival*, with theater, ballet, concerts and folk dancing in the Odeon and in Paphos Fort. **August**: During the two week long *Pampafia* exhibition in the park on Messogis Avenue, craftsmen from the Paphos area display their work. **Last weekend in August**: *Wine Festival* in the village of Stroumbi on the road to Polis. **End of November**: Half-marathon in Paphos, organised by the Cyprus Health Runner's Club, tel. / fax 420559.

Central Post Office, with poste restante and afternoon service: Themidos St., tel. 232241. In Nea Paphos: Ayios Antonios Street.

Emergency: Dial 199 for **Paphos Hospital**, Neophytou Nikolaidi St. In Ktima: tel. 240100.

BUSES: Within the city and to the nearby villages of Emba, Lemba, Kissonerga, Peyia and Yeroskipos as well as to the Ayios Neophytos Monastery and to the airport numerous times daily, leaving from the market hall and many other bus stops (Alepa Bus Co., Nikodemou Mylona St. 28, tel. 234410). Buses to Limassol and Nikosia Mon-Sat 3-5 x daily (Alepa Bus Co. and Kemek/Nea Amoroza Bus Co., Pallikaridis St. 79, tel. 236822). Buses run to Polis up to 11 times daily (Kemek/Nea Amoroza Bus Co.).

RENTAL CARS: **Andy Spyrou/Europcar**, Poseidonos Ave., Natalia Court, tel. 241850. **A. Petsas & Sons**, Apostle Paul Ave. 86, Green Court, tel. 235522. **Budget Rent a Car**, Tombs of the Kings Road, Dora Complex, tel. 253824. **Hertz**, Apostle Paul Ave. 54A, tel. 233985.

Leos/Thrifty, corner of Poseidonos Ave./Iason St., tel. 233770. **Sea Island Car Rental**, Tombs of the Kings Road 26, tel. 231456. **Sir Rentals**, Ellados St. 94, tel. 242258. **Geko**, Vladimirou Irakleous St. 10, tel. 232848. *SERVICE (GROUP) TAXIS*: **Karydas/Kyriakos**, tel. 232459. **Kypros**, tel. 237722. **Makris**, tel. 232538.

Nea Paphos has many boutiques with fashionable beach wear and traditional handicrafts. Paphos District is famed for its basketry and wickerwork, once produced in almost every village but now only continued in a few, including Mesoyi and Yeroskipos.

CORAL BAY

Queen's Bay, Coral Bay Road, tel. 246600, fax 246777. **Cynthiana Beach**, Coral Bay Road, 8 km northwest of Paphos, tel. 233900, fax 244648. **Yeronisos**, Ayios Yeoryios, Peyia, tel. / fax 621078.

Kissonerga: **Lobster Tavern**, 6 km from Coral Bay, tel. 243940, good seafood dishes. **John's Tavern**, tel. 234205, good *sephtalia* (grilled sausage) and meat dishes. Peyia: **Vrissi Taverna**, 4 km from Coral Bay, tel. 621113, for *meze* and great fish.

POLIS / LACHI REGION (☎ 06)

Cyprus Tourism Organisation, Ayiou Nikolaou St. 1 (by the market hall), Polis, tel. 322468.

Anassa, Neo Chorio, tel. 233550, fax 231656. **Elia Lachi Holiday Village**, Lachi, tel. 321 011, fax 322024. **Droushia Heights**, Drousha, tel. 332351, fax 332353. **Lover's Nest**, Polis, tel. 322 401, fax 322440. **Souli**, Neo Chorio, tel. 321088, fax 322474. **Aphrodite Beach**, Neo Chorio, tel. 3210 01, fax 322015. **Chrysafina**, Prodhromi, tel. 321180, fax 322465. **Latsi**, Lachi, tel. 321411, fax 321468.

Polis Camping, tel. 321526, situated by the beach, in a eucalyptus grove, open March to November.

There are a number of good tavernas and restaurants concentrated around the village square in Polis, close to the market hall. Good country fare is offered in the tavernas in the villages of Drousha and Neo Chorio, situated just above the coast. For fish, it is best to head to one of the tavernas at the harbor of Lachi.

PAPHOS FOREST

Rest House, Stavros tis Psokas, tel. 722338, 7 rooms with shower and fireplace (reservations will be necessary). **Oniro**, Panayia, tel. 722434, fax 722929.

Birth house of Archbishop Makarios in Panayia: The keys can be picked up at the Makarios exhibition in the Cultural Centre by the Makarios monument, open daily 9 am-1 pm and 3-6 pm.

Paphos

DIVIDED CAPITAL

NICOSIA
NICOSIA DISTRICT
TROODOS MOUNTAINS
MARATHASA VALLEY
MAKHERAS MONASTERY

Nicosia

NICOSIA

Nicosia ❶ is the capital of Cyprus and its largest city. It is the center of government as well as business and cultural life. Greater Nicosia has a population of 190,000, of which 160,000 live in the south and 30,000 in the north.

In historical terms, Nicosia is a comparatively new city. The only remains of the Bronze Age ancient city called *Ledra* or *Lydra* are a supposed acropolis near the main government complex, and rock tombs which developers stumble across from time to time when digging foundations. Copper-producing and smelting centers such as Idalion and Tamassos nearby were far more important, as were the ports of Kition (present-day Larnaca), Paphos and Salamis. Lefkosia, as it is still called by Greek Cypriots today, became the administrative capital of the island in the 10th century when the Byzantine rulers moved the seat of government from Constantia (now Salamis). After Richard the Lionheart and his crusaders wrested the island from the usurper Isaac Comnenos in the 12th century, Cyprus came under the rule of Frankish lords. They set up the Lusignan Dynasty which

Left: The younger generation is full of enthusiasm and optimism.

ruled Cyprus for nearly 300 years. For the Lusignans, Lefkosia became known as Nicosia, and it was under their rule that it developed into a rich and lovely city of palaces, gardens and churches, and boasted breathtaking Gothic and Renaissance architecture equal in beauty to that of Europe.

Many of the buildings and gardens of the Lusignans, which stretched out on both sides of the Pedieos River, were razed by the Venetians in 1567. The threat of Ottoman attack on the last bastion of Christendom in the eastern Mediterranean had become very strong, and the Venetians made a last-minute attempt to fortify the island's main towns. Venetian experts felt Nicosia was practically indefensible, sprawled as it was in the middle of a plain with weak city walls and eight gates, and would have preferred to abandon it and fortify only the city of Famagusta. A scarcity of building materials led engineers to destroy many fine buildings, including 80 churches, numerous monasteries and the Cornelian Palace built by Marco Cornaro – the father of Caterina Cornaro, the last queen of Cyprus – and the remains of these were used as fortifying material to reduce Nicosia to a tight-walled city with a circumference of just five kilometers. Though they may have been hastily raised, these new Vene-

Map pp. 64-65, City Map pp. 58-59, Info pp. 70-71

55

tian Walls were in fact a perfect feat of military engineering.

The city did fall to the Ottoman army after all, in 1570, and many of the catholic churches were converted into mosques, whereas many of the smaller Greek churches were permitted to continue serving the Greek Orthodox population. In time, whatever was left of these destroyed buildings was used again in the restoration and extension of other buildings. This created utter confusion for historians who later researched these buildings. They found inexplicable features, such as Gothic lintels and sometimes even sarcophagi, built into structures of a much later date.

During the period of Ottoman occupation, Nicosia, like the rest of the island, went into decline. The governor of the island had moved into the old Palace of the Provveditore (Venetian: Lieutenant), the palace of the former Venetian governor, now called the *Konak* or *Saray*. On the whole, there were few attempts made to rebuild or even maintain the once-splendid Gothic majesty of the city's buildings.

When the British acquired the island in 1878, they initially made do with the buildings already available to them. It was not until 1931 that they raised an impressive two-storied stone building with a giant British coat of arms dominating the entrance. This is now the Presidential Palace.

In the middle of the 1900s, Nicosia began spreading out towards the nearby villages and into the countryside. By the time of Cyprus' independence in 1960, many of these villages were suburbs of the city. There were no clearly defined quarters where Greeks or Turks lived, though there were areas within the city walls where one or the other community

Right: Unfortunately a relaxed stroll through the lanes of Nicosia has it's limits - namely those of the Green Line.

was dominant. Delineation of areas was more by trade than nationality: goldsmiths, carpenters and textile shops were all found on their own particular streets. The main market near Ayia Sophia attracted whole streets of retailers, while Konak Square accommodated mainly bookshops and car showrooms. Outside the city walls, Nicosia was still mainly residential. Larnaca Street, now bustling, broad, shop-lined and called Makarios III Avenue, used to be a quiet residential area of townhouses amid gardens.

The Division of Nicosia

The division of Nicosia began in 1963, immediately after the intercommunal troubles between the two ethnic groups became evident. British officers, who had been called in to supervise the negotiations between the combatants, drew a cease-fire line across Nicosia with a green pen, which would become known as the "Green Line." It ran from the Paphos Gate down Paphos Street and Hermes Street to just north of the Famagusta Gate, with a similar line further northwards across the suburbs. Due to this arbitrary delineation, the central post office, law courts, the Kyrenia Gate police station, the land survey office, as well as many other government offices, hundreds of businesses and residences, a flour mill, factories and entire new housing districts in Kermia, Constantia and Neapolis, the suburb of Omorphita, and the Armenian Quarter, with its church, school, social clubs and family homes around Victoria Street were now all in the Turkish sector. The main road to Kyrenia was also cut off.

Since medieval times, the northern coast with Kyrenia and the castles of St. Hilarion and Kantara in the Pentadaktylos Range were popular summer retreats. Cutting off the road to Kyrenia meant the Nicosians now had to travel to their favorite seaside resort (until

Nicosia

then a mere 25 minute drive away) by United Nations escorted convoy, which could take nearly an hour. Eventually, a new road to Kyrenia bypassing the Turkish enclave was built over the Pentadaktylos Range. In Nicosia itself, development now moved to the south.

It appeared that the Turkish invasion of 1974 had sounded the knell for Old Nicosia as a commercial and business center. The Green Line became the nucleus of confrontation with its armed soldiers and a wall of sandbags; this was a desolate area of no man's land surrounded by residential districts in which the prevalent feeling was tension. As Greater Nicosia grew, the Old Town seemed to shrink more and more into itself. This trend was reversed in the early 1980s, when the progressive Mayor Lellos Demetriades and his Municipal Council set up a plan to revitalize the Old Town.

Two districts, which were the focal points of this planned change, were Laiki Yitonia, initially a tiny pedestrian area

with a few restored old houses, and the area surrounding the Famagusta Gate, which was itself being used as a storeroom by the Department of Antiquities. In the meantime, work had already started on a unified sewage system for the city across the line, which took in the Greek and Turkish sectors and was backed by the United Nations Development Program. The plan for revitalizing Old Nicosia was incorporated in another UN-backed project, the Nicosia Master Plan, in which the two halves of the city would be restored in a cohesive and homogenous style. Laiki Yitonia was an immediate success, and now covers five times its original area, with more and more streets being turned into pedestrian areas annually. The Famagusta Gate with its wide arched passage through the Venetian walls and adjoining stone guard rooms, was restored and turned into the Nicosia Municipal Cultural Center.

Most places of interest in southern Nicosia are found either inside the walled city or just outside of it; all are practically within walking distance of each other. If you are driving in from another town, park your car in the municipal parking area in the moat below the Town Hall, the entrance of which off Stasinos Avenue is clearly marked. Steps at the far end of the moat will lead you onto the ramparts near the post office and into Eleftheria (Liberty) Square. It is best to visit the Cyprus Museum, the Byzantine Museum, the Folk Art Museum and the House of the Dragoman in the mornings. In the afternoons, the first three are open for only two or three hours, while the House of the Dragoman remains closed.

Getting Around The Old Town

It is usually best to explore Nicosia by starting at **Eleftheria Square**. This is where Nicosia'a main shopping street, **Ledra Street**, begins. To the right of Ledra Street, the restored old town quarter of ****Laiki Yitonia** stretches out, with its pedestrian zone, pretty houses, numerous tavernas and stores full of handicrafts, as well as one particularly well-stocked bookstore specializing in literature on Cyprus. On **Hippocrates Street** you will come to the **Leventis Municipal Museum ❶**, recently awarded the European Museum Prize by the European Council. The museum occupies one of three houses built by a prosperous Nicosian in 1885 for his daughters. It was acquired by the Anastasios G. Leventis Foundation in the 1980s and lovingly restored it to its former glory. The history of the city is told retrospectively through artifacts, jewelry, coins, maps, posters and costumes and an ancient tomb, which was found in the cellar during restoration: starting with the Nicosia of the present day, the retrospective leads you through the history of the city, step by step. Admission is free of charge, but small donations are always welcome.

The privately-run **Jewelry Museum ❷** on nearby Praxippos Street can also be

viewed without charge. Not only typical Cypriot silver jewelry is displayed in the two small exhibition rooms, but also silver tableware, as it still exists in many of the households on the island today.

Exiting Laiki Yitonia onto the ramparts, turn left and go down Konstantinos Paleologou Street to **Canning Bridge** *(Gefyra Kannigkos)*. If it is market day (usually Wednesday), the area will be crammed with stalls selling fruit, vegetables and other goods, and the carts of traveling peddlers. On the The **Bairaktar Mosque ❸** rises above the **Costanza Bastion** closeby. The mosque was built by the Ottomans in memory of the standard bearer who fell here during the attack on Nicosia in 1570. Via Areos Street

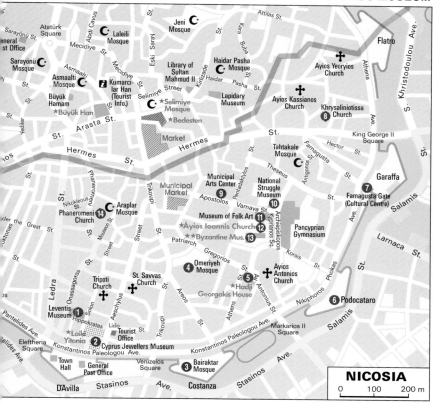

Nicosia

take a northerly direction to the **Omeriye Mosque** ❹, formerly the 14th century Church of St. Mary of the Augustinians.

Walk beside the mosque, still a prayer temple for Moslems resident in southern Nicosia, up Patriarch Gregorios Street to the House of the Dragoman on the right hand side. The ***House of Hadji Georgakis Kornesios** ❺, its official name, is the most important preserved example of urban architecture of the last century of Ottoman rule in Old Nicosia.

Hadji Georgakis Kornesios was the "Dragoman of Cyprus" (*dragoman* literally means "interpreter"), the highest rank held by a Greek layman from 1779/80 to 1805. The Archbishop, as ethnarch (leader of the Greek Cypriot nation),

looked after the spiritual and temporal wellbeing of the Greeks of Cyprus, whereas the Dragoman was the liaison with the Ottoman authorities, responsible for tax collecting and other administrative functions.

From the street, the house looks rather fortress-like with its thick walls and iron-barred windows. But this outer appearance is deceiving. Once inside the main walls, the house takes on a completely different aspect. There are the colonnades and courtyard of a typically prosperous villa of the period, with auxiliary and service rooms on the ground floor and the living quarters above. At the bottom of the garden, beyond the courtyard with its fountain, is the *hamam*, the family's per-

59

sonal Turkish bath, complete with a heating system under the floor. The living quarters have been furnished in the early 20th century style of grand town houses. A long corridor leads to the decorated "divan room," the only one of the Ottoman Period still preserved in Cyprus. Here the Dragoman would receive his guests, who lounged on the lavish coverings and cushions of the low divans.

Walking along Nikiphoros Phokas Avenue, past the **Podocataro Bastion** ❻ with its impressive sculptures called the *Liberation of Cyprus*, you will come to **Famagusta Gate** ❼. The *Porta Giuliana*, as it was once called, was the strongest of the three Venetian gates. Since its restoration, it houses the **Cultural Center**.

Further along the rampart street, now known as Athena Avenue, and turning

Above: If the abundant fruit and vegetable ranges at the street stalls do not suffice, don't miss a visit to the country market at Costanzo Bastion on Wednesdays. Right: Statue of Makarios III in front of the new Archbishopric.

back towards town again at King George II Square, you reach the Khrysaliniotissa quarter. The adobe houses here with their characteristic bay windows are currently undergoing restoration and are being rented out to young families, so that this quarter, neglected due to its proximity to the *Green Line*, may once again be infused with new life.

The quarter is named for **Khrysaliniotissa Church** ❽, Nicosia's oldest Byzantine church, dedicated to "Our Lady of the Golden Flax". This beautiful domed church is said to have been built by Queen Helena Palaeologa and contains many noteworthy icons, some of which date back to the 1300s.

Returning to the western part of the Old Town, you cross Hermes Street (Odos Ermou) and turn off into Pentadaktylos Street. On one of its side streets, to the right, you will see the old electrical works. Today, this building houses the **Municipal Arts Center** ❾, with its somewhat avant-garde exhibition rooms. Temporary exhibitions here pres-

ent the works of leading contemporary Cypriot and international artists.

At the other end of Apostolos Varnava Street with its Municipal Art Gallery, two further interesting collections are available for viewing: the **National Struggle Museum** ⑩ (EOKA Museum), which contains various relics of the 1955-1959 Liberation Struggle, and the **Folk Art Museum** ⑪, which is located in residence of the Orthodox Archbishop. It used to be the Benedictine Abbey of St. John the Evangelist, but passed into the hands of the Greek Orthodox Church when the Benedictine Order left the island after the Mameluke raid of 1426, and was a monastery until the 18th century.

The Byzantine-style **New Archbishopric** was completed in 1960. A gigantic **Statue of Archbishop Makarios III** (which was ordered by his successor Archbishop Khrysostomos) dominates the forecourt. Walk along the railings to the open courtyard which leads to the small ***Church of Ayios Ioannis** ⑫, which despite its size is in actual fact the official cathedral of Nicosia. Built in 1662, its interior was painted in the years between 1736 and 1756. Both Byzantine and Western elements are evident in Biblical scenes, while the story of the discovery, in Salamis, of the tomb of St. Barnabas, who was the founder of the Cypriot Church, is depicted in late-Byzantine style. Once again, parts of other buildings were used in the builing of this church. Over the western entrance is a sculpted marble panel from some destroyed Gothic building, with the Lusignan coat of arms. Another coat of arms appears above the door, as well as a further sculpted marble panel over the southern doorway, carved in Italian Renaissance style. A 15th century sarcophagus has been embedded in the back porch.

The ****Byzantine Museum** ⑬ is in the courtyard behind the Ayios Ioannis Cathedral, and it belongs to the Archbishop Makarios III Cultural Foundation. One of the most exceptional collections of Byzantine icons and murals in the world, it covers the entire spectrum of Byzantine

art in Cyprus from the 5th to the 18th centuries. The oldest objects in the museum are six Early Christian mosaics from the 5th century, depicting representations of Mary and the Apostles. They were originally housed in the Panagia Kanakaria Church near Lythrankomi in the Turkish part of the island, but were stolen from there in 1974 and reappeared in 1989 through an American art dealer. The Church of Cyprus successfully sued the U.S. for the unconditional return of the stolen goods. The oldest icon in the museum hangs just beyond the entrance (No. 1). It is a fragment of a painting of Mary executed in encaustic technique from the 8th or 9th century. In this early method of icon painting, egg yolk was not used as a fixer for the pigment, as was later common practice, but rather, honey. Because of this, the color texture is somewhat reminiscent of Impressionist paintings.

Above: Byzantine frescoes in the Church of Ayios Ioannis. Right: Cyprus Museum - a bronze statue of Emperor Septimius Severus.

The route to the sights around Paphos Gate should be taken via Phaneromeni Street, at the northern end of the pedestrian zone. **Phaneromeni Church ⑭** dates back to 1872 and was erected on the site of an older Greek Orthodox monastery or convent, with stones taken from the ruins of Athalassa Castle just outside the city. At the back of the churchyard is a marble **Mausoleum dedicated to Archbishop Kyprianos**, his bishops and other Greek Cypriot leaders who were killed on July 9, 1821, by order of the Turkish Governor Küchük Mehmed. They were either beheaded or hanged. The reason for this was that the struggle for freedom against the Turks had broken out in Greece some three months earlier. The Governor wanted to set a brutal example, so that Cyprus would not follow suit.

Around Paphos Gate

The ***Cyprus Museum ⑮** on Museum Street is the most outstanding archaeological museum in the Republic of Cyprus. A first-time visitor to the museum may find it difficult to absorb so much history, but will still marvel at the beauty and artistry of works created up to 8,500 years ago.

Enter Room I and proceed counter-clockwise around the ground floor. The displays are arranged chronologically and typologically. Please bear in mind that objects may be on loan to another institution, or may have been moved to another room, so that the following description may not always match the current layout.

Room I: Aceramic and Ceramic Neolithic (7000-3750 B.C.) to Chalcolithic (3500-2500/2300 B.C.) Periods. Stone figurines and implements of stone, flint and bone; human figures with simple features; pottery, jewelry and steatite cross figures from the Ceramic Neolithic and Chalcolithic Periods.

Room II: Early Bronze Age (Early Cypriot, 2300-1900 B.C.). Clay figurines, plank figures, terra cotta models of a plowing and ritual scene.

Room III: Pottery from the Middle Bronze Age (Middle Cypriot, 1900-1625 B.C.) to the Hellenic Period. A faience rhyton (ancient drinking horn of pottery or bronze) from Mycenaean times is especially beautiful. In two of the three frieze panels lively scenes in inlay or enamel can be seen: in the upper panel two bulls, an antelope and a wild goat are racing past; beneath this, two young men can be seen, each hunting a bull. A Cypriot speciality is the so-called "free field style" painted vase from the Cypro-Archaic Period (700-600 B.C.). On one of the loveliest of these vases, a mighty bull can be seen sniffing a lotus flower.

Room IV: **Votive figures from Ayia Irini,** Late Bronze Age (Late Cypriot, 1625-1050 B.C.). Warriors, bulls, centaurs, etc., miniature to life-size.

Rooms V, VI, XIII: Sculpture from the Cypro-Archaic (750-475 B.C.) to Roman (58 B.C.-A.D. 330) Periods, showing de-

velopment from monumental, stiff, stylized works with Oriental and Egyptian influences, to classical Greek and finally Hellenistic styles. In addition there are Roman realistic portraits, the famous Torso of **Aphrodite of Soli**, and a larger-than-life **bronze statue of Emperor Septimus Severus**.

Room VII: The most beautiful and, artistically-speaking, valuable examples of Cypriot bronze casting have been gathered together here and they include famous statues of deities including one of the **Horned God of Enkomi** (a finding from northern Cyprus). In addition, there are a number of Roman mosaics, including the well-known one of Leda and the Swan from the ancient Temple of Aphrodite in Kouklia. Furthermore, there are a number of display cases containing marvelous jewelry. One of the cases has a golden scepter, found in Kourion, with a cloisonné orb; on its tip a pair of bearded vultures are poised. An interesting necklace from the seventh century is made of dainty pearls, counterbalanced by a cylin-

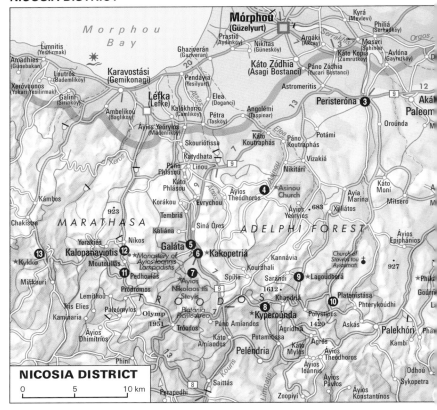

drical agate pendant crowned by a golden bee and two serpents. Portions of the famous **silver treasure of Lapithos** (now Lambousa in northern Cyprus) from pre-Christian times can also be seen here.

Basement Level, Rooms IX and X: In Room IX gravestones from the sixth to third century B.C. are predominantly on display. In Room X you will see numerous inscriptions in Cypro-Minoan syllabic script; a script which has never been deciphered and which was in use until the Hellenic Age.

Upper Level with Room XI: Furniture with ivory inlay work, and bronze objects from a royal tomb in Salamis (Northern Cyprus) from the eighth century B.C. In an unnumbered side room the history and technique of copper mining and copper working are clearly documented.

Room XIV: Middle Bronze Age plank idols and small terra cotta figures.

Diagonally across the road is the neoclassical **Municipal Theater** ⑯, from 1967, behind which the **Municipal Gardens** stretch out. North of the **Paphos Gate** ⑰ and **Statue of Markos Drakos** - one of the heroes of the 1955-59 Liberation Struggle against British rule, and further along the Venetian Walls and the **Roccas Bastion**, Turkish flags are prominently displayed, signalling the boundaries of the *Green Line*. You then reach the **Ledra Palace Checkpoint** ⑱, the only point at which the Green Line can be crossed into Northern Cyprus (see "Entry

to visit a number of the sights mentioned above. Some mountain villages have unique painted churches, outstanding examples of a remarkable indigenous art form. Almost all of them are kept locked, however, and finding the priest or caretaker who has the key can be a time-consuming process, but it often leads to pleasant encounters with friendly villagers who are usually more than eager to show guests something of their cultural heritage.

FROM NICOSIA TO TROODOS

The route from Nicosia to Troodos leads down Grivas Dighenis Avenue to the traffic lights at **Kykko Metokhi ❷**, a dependency of Kykko Monastery built in 1890. Turn left and follow the road signs for Troodos through the straggling new suburbs of **Anthoupolis** and **Archangelos**, as far as the access road to the new highway.

At **Kokkini Trimithia** you meet the old access road again, which bypasses most of the villages. You will see on your left the villages of **Akaki** and then **Peristerona ❸**, which appears on either side of a wide dry riverbed. In the distance you can clearly see the Byzantine **Church of Saints Barnabas and Hilarion**, built in the early 10th century with 17th to 18th century additions. It is one of the two surviving five-domed Cypriot churches (the other is in Yeroskipos). Its restored iconostasis, dating back to 1549, has a colorful icon, the *Presentation in the Temple*. An adjacent **mosque**, formerly a church, shows this was once a mixed village in which Greek and Turkish Cypriots lived in harmony, side by side.

**Asinou Church

At **Kato Koutraphas** turn left on to a country road. Via **Nikitari** you will reach ****Asinou Church ❹**, also known as

Requirements," page 84). A Cypriot Police checkpoint precedes the no man's land controlled by the UN in front of the former Ledra Palace Hotel, and further on, the northern Cyprus checkpoint.

NICOSIA DISTRICT

Nicosia District is the largest district of the island and includes all of the Solea and Marathasa valleys, and parts of the Pitsilia region, with picturesque mountain villages, fruit orchards, hill resorts and countless Byzantine churches and monasteries - a contrast to the villages and ancient sites in the plains. On a day trip from Nicosia or Limassol, either with a tour group or by rented car, it is possible

Panayia Phorviotissa, with some of the finest examples of Byzantine mural paintings on the entire island. If the church is not open, stop at Nikitari to find out about getting the key.

Asinou Church, now on UNESCO's list of World Cultural Heritage Sites, is dedicated to the Virgin Mary. It is a rectangular vaulted building with a steep-pitched roof of flat tiles, and its interior is completely painted in brilliant Byzantine style. Over the south entrance you will see a painting of the sponsor, identified as Nikephoros Magister, offering a model of the church (looking very much as it does today) to the Virgin Mary. From the various inscriptions, experts believe that the church was built between the years 1099 and 1105. About two-thirds of the original decoration in the very classical and courtly Comnenian style (1081-1185) has survived, with some excellent

Above: Asinou Church with its characteristic steep-pitched roof. Right: Houses with roofed wooden balconies in Kakopetria.

examples of how the artists of the period portrayed various incidents in the lives of Jesus and the Virgin Mary, such as the *Annunciation*, Christ's *Triumphal Entry into Jerusalem*, the *Last Supper* and the *Death of the Virgin Mary*, as well as the obligatory depictions of the saints. The *Communion of the Apostles* in the center of the apse is one of the most interesting compositions in this style, showing Christ offering wine to six of the apostles, with his gaze directed at Judas, who has turned away at the extreme right. The northwest recess is dominated with a very interesting painting: the *Forty Martyrs of Sebaste*. This is a scene from early Christian times, and legend has it that the martyrs were forced on to a frozen lake and then tempted to forsake their religion by succumbing to hot baths which had been set up on the shore.

Return to the main road via the same route, leading through the foothills of the Troodos Mountains to a road junction. At this junction take a right-hand turn toward Kalopanayiotis and Kykko.

Galata and *Kakopetria

After passing through Evrychou, Tembria and Kaliana, follow a sign for Galata and Kakopetria, which are now practically one village. The road through these villages is rather narrow, and in summer drivers need a great deal of patience to cope with the creeping traffic.

In the middle of **Galata ❺** stands the **Church of Ayios Sozomenos**, dating back to the early 16th century. It has a steep-pitched roof and a complete series of frescoes comprising several cycles. One cycle depicts the life of Christ, scenes from the life of the Virgin Mary, and episodes from the life of St. George, including the *Slaying of the Dragon*. Also inside are paintings of various individual saints and female martyrs, while the exterior north wall has two paintings: the *Seven Ecumenical Councils of the Church* and the *Triumph of Orthodoxy*.

The **Church of the Archangel Michael** was originally called Panayia Theotokos (Mary Mother of God) and is completely painted in the post-Byzantine style which was typical of the early 16th century.

Nearby is the larger **Church of Panayia Podithou**, which once belonged to a monastery. It was erected in 1502, and contains paintings of the Italo-Byzantine style, which were popular at that time.

Drive over the small bridge to *Kakopetria ❻. Follow the sign for the *Old Village*. The upper path leads past the "bad rocks" which give the village its name (*kako* is Greek for "bad," and *petra* means "stone"). The cobbled alleys between the balconied stone houses wind gently above the river, which is just below. On the other side of the river you can see the picturesque **Mill Restaurant**, which is built into the rock near the original Old Mill. This is the perfect place to stop and savor delicious freshly-caught trout.

The most beautiful church in the Solea Valley is *Ayios Nikolaos tis Steyis ❼ (St. Nicholas of the Roof), five kilometers southwest of Kakopetriawa. It was erected in the early 11th century, and a domed narthex was added one century later. The distinctive steep-pitched roof of flat tiles was added on early, intended as a protection against snow and rain, and thus gave its name to the church. Paintings from the 11th to 17th centuries cover the church's whole interior, providing vivid examples of the various changes in style and technique during this period. Some of the later paintings were removed to reveal earlier ones. The earliest, such as the *Raising of Lazarus* and the *Triumphal Entry into Jerusalem*, are in the west vault.

To *Panayia tou Araka Church

Exit the highway and drive eastwards to *Kyperounda ❽. Its **Stavros Church** is worth seeing, as its 16th century chapel has a rich collection of paintings.

From Kyperounda, take the road to Khandria and **Lagoudhera ❾** to the ***Church of Panayia tou Araka**. The 12th century church is just outside the village on the road to Sarandi. Visitors can ask for the key and be escorted through the church by the priest, who may be found on the premises next door. The interior of this church has the most complete series of paintings from the mid-Byzantine Period on the island. The *Christ* in the dome is one of the most beautiful versions of the subject.

From Laguoudhera, continue on to the village of **Platanistassa ❿**. There you can inquire in the first café on the main street as to the whereabouts of the key to the idyllically-set **Church of Stavros tou Ayiasmati**. Inside this steep-pitched tile roof church there are some 40 frescoes from around the year 1500 to be seen.

MARATHASA VALLEY
From Kakopetria to the Kykko Monastery

Kakopetria (**❻**) is a good place from which to explore the western Troodos region. Leave the highway in Troodos village, which is at the foot of the 1951 meter high Olymp (for the hike from Troodos see page 34), heading toward **Prodomos**. The road then winds through **Pedhoulas ⓫**, a summer resort famous for its cherries, and **Moutoullas**, with its **Chapel of Panayia tou Moutoullas**, built in 1280.

Kalopanayiotis ⓬, the lowest-lying of the three Marathasa Valley villages, is famous for its sulphur springs and the ***Monastery of Ayios Ioannis Lampadistis**. Its church complex is a combination of buildings of various eras: an 11th century church dedicated to St. Herakleidios on the south; a vaulted

Right: The Church of Ayios Ioannis Lampadistis is a treasure trove of Byzantine art.

church dedicated to Ayios Ioannis Lampadistis in the middle (renovated in the 18th century); a timber-roofed narthex attached along the west end of the two churches in the mid-15th century; and a tall vaulted building on the north, attached at the end of the 15th century, which might have been a Latin chapel. The whole building is covered by a second protective roof of flat tiles.

In the **Church of Ayios Herakleidios** there are 13th century paintings in the dome, the south vault and in the western arm of the nave. The *Triumphal Entry into Jerusalem* is preserved in vivid color in the western vault. There is a pretty depiction of children among a date palm.

The **Church of Ayios Ioannis Lampadistis**, in the middle of the complex, was rebuilt at the beginning of the 18th century retaining the northeast pier over the saint's tomb. A narrow arch in the east has fragments of two layers of paintings, suggesting a 12th century date for the original church. The skull of the saint is preserved in a silver casket above the tomb and is believed to have healing powers. The fame of the holy relic always attracted many pilgrims and by the 15th century, the monastery was extended by a vaulted narthex, which later collapsed but was rebuilt again in timber. But the paintings, including the *Miracles of Christ*, the *Disciples at the Holy Sepulcher,* the *Resurrection* and the *Last Judgment* located on the north, east and south walls, survived. An inscription identifies the artist as coming from Constantinople, most probably after the Turks captured it in 1453.

The **Latin Chapel** contains the most complete series of frescoes in the Italo-Byzantine style very popular on the island 500 years ago.

*Kykko Monastery ⓭ is the most famous and richest monastery in Cyprus, and is reached on a relatively good road either via Pedhoulas or via Yerakies north of Kalopanayiotis.

The first President of Cyprus, Archbishop Makarios, served here as a novice, as did the present Archbishop. The monastery was founded around 1100, during the reign of Byzantine Emperor Alexios Comnenos. According to tradition, it was established by a monk called Isaias, with the generous payment he had received from the emperor for curing the his daughter of sciatica. Whether it was also Isaias who brought the famous *Icon of the Virgin Mary*, which is said to have been painted by St. Luke and is actually one of only three surviving works of his, is not certain. Enclosed in a shrine made of tortoise shell and mother-of-pearl, it stands in front of the iconostasis, and is only brought out on particularly special occasions.

The monastery owns several priceless icons and sacred objects, some of which have apparently come from Russia, transported by pilgrims on their way to the Holy Land or from Russian Orthodox churches with which the monastery had close relations.

Three kilometers west of is **Throni tis Panayias** (Throne of the Mother of God), where Archbishop Makarios was buried, at his own request, not far from his home village of Panayia.

August 15 and September 8 are the most important dates for religious festivals taking place in Kykko.

FROM NICOSIA TO THE MAKHERAS MONASTERY

In Nicosia, drive through Evagoras and Demosthenis Severis Avenues, past the Presidential Palace and the roundabout, head southwards down the broad highway via **Strovolos** and **Lakatamia**, and follow signs to Dheftera and Pera. 11 kilometers out of Nicosia you will see a signpost for the **Panayia Khrysospiliotissa Church** ❹ (Our Lady of the Golden Cave). This is a catacomb which was enlarged to make a church in early Christian times.

Beyond Kato Dheftera keep left, driving towards Pera. At the village of

Episkopeion turn off to **Politiko** ⓯. This small and very pretty village stands on the former site of **Tamassos**, a city-kingdom of ancient Cyprus and an important copper center. Excavations here have uncovered the **Royal Tombs** and a **temple** dedicated to a female deity, either Astarte or Aphrodite, as well as the remains of what have been identified as copper workshops.

About 500 meters further is *★Ayios **Herakleidios Monastery**. It is said that when St. Paul and St. Barnabas came to Cyprus, they were guided to Tamassos by Herakleidios, whom they later ordained as Bishop of Tamassos. He was martyred at the age of 60 and laid to rest in his cave, where he used lived and preached. The monastery, founded in A.D. 400, contains his skull, and is decorated with fine frescoes and icons. The nuns who have resided here since 1962 sell honey and marzipan.

Return now to Episkopeion and continue on to the **Makheras Monastery** ⓰, via Pera and Kambia. It was founded by two monks in 1148, when an icon of the Virgin Mary was discovered in a nearby cave. The monks are not very fond of seeing non-Orthodox visitors; tour groups and those who are improperly dressed will not be allowed inside.

Nearby is a **Monument to Grigoris Afxentiou**, an EOKA fighter who was killed in the 1955-59 Liberation Struggle.

Continue further to Lazania, where the road begins to ascend again, and take the turning signposted for *★Phikardou* ⓱. This small village, in its entirety, has been declared an "ancient monument." Traditional activities such as threshing and the production of wine and *zivania* continue to this day. If you can, pay a visit to the **Katsinioros House**, now the local museum at the northern edge of the village. Returning to the road, take a right turn and a short distance after **Gourri** you will be back on the main road to Klirou and Nicosia.

NICOSIA (☎ 02)

🛈 **Cyprus Tourism Organisation**, Laiki Yitonia, east of Eleftheria Square, tel. 444264.

🛏 ⑤⑤⑤ **Cyprus Hilton**, Arch. Makarios III. Ave. 116, tel. 377777, fax 377788, restaurants, pool, gym, jogging and squash. **Holiday Inn**, Regaena St. 70, tel. 475131, fax 473337, only luxury hotel in the Old Town, indoor pool. ⑤⑤ **Asty Hotel**, Prince Charles St. 12, Ayios Dhometios, tel. 773030, fax 773311. **Best Western Classic**, Regaena St. 94, tel. 464006, fax 360072, on the city wall. **Cleopatra Hotel**, Florina St. 8, tel. 445254, fax 452618, centrally located, comfortable bar beside the pool, good restaurant. **Europa Hotel**, Alkaio St. 16, Enkomi, tel. 454537, fax 474417. ⑤ **Averof Hotel**, Averof St. 19, tel. 773447, fax 773411, friendly family-style hotel in a quiet neighborhood. **Rimi**, Solonos St. 5, tel. 43153, fax 452816, in Laiki Yitonia. **Royal**, Euripides St. 17, tel. 463245, the most basic and least expensive hotel in town. **Venetian Walls**, Ouzonian St. 38, tel. 450805, fax 473 337, on the city wall. *YOUTH HOSTEL:* Hadjidaki St. 5, tel. 442027, open daily from 7:30 am-10 pm and 4-11 pm. **Cyprus Youth Hostels Association**, tel. 442027 (days), tel. 446542 (evenings).

✖ **LAIKI YITONIA:** A variety of restaurants, tavernas and bars serve good local food and *meze*. **Archontiko**, 27 Aristokyprou, tel. 450080, outdoor seating when the weather is good. **Xefoto**, 6 Aeschylos St., tel. 477840, excellent Greek music ever evening, which often inspires customers to dance. **FAMAGUSTA GATE:** Piano bars, theater-restaurants, tavernas with music and gyros-restaurants. Many of them are run by artists and actors with their own local following. **MAKEDONITISSA:** This area off Grivas Dighenis Avenue is bustling with tavernas and bouzouki nightspots.

EUROPEAN CUISINE: **Scorpios**, Stassinos St. 1, Enkomi, near the Europa Hotel, tel. 351850, exclusive restaurant offering haute cuisine, reservation essential. **Corona**, Orpheus St. 15 A, Ayios Dhometios, tel. 444223. **Mignon**, Metokhi St. 38, near the Churchill Hotel, tel. 781032. **Navarino**, Navarino St. 1, tel. 450775. *EUROPEAN AND GREEK CUISINE:* **Date Restaurant**, corner of Khalkokondylos St./Agathon St., near the Hilton Hotel, tel. 376737, sophisticated *meze*, popular with business people, reservation essential. **Ekali**, Ayios Spyridhon St. 1, Pallouriotissa, tel. 433950, panoramic view of Nicosia from the rooftop restaurant. *FISH TAVERNAS:* **Astakos**, Menelaos St., Enkomi, tel. 351917. **Kavouri**, Strovolos Ave. 125, Strovolos, tel. 425153, closed on Sundays **Psarolimano**, 28th October Ave. 55,

Makedonitissa, tel. 350990. *CHINESE*: **Changs,** Acropolis St. 1, Enkomi, near the Ledra Hotel, tel. 351350. **Pagoda,** Loukis Akritas St. 11, tel. 771000. *CYPRIOT MEZE:* **Mandri Tavern,** Arch. Kyprianou Ave. 27, Strovolos, tel. 497200.

📺 **Mythos Pub,** Theodotou St. **Maple Leaf Pub,** Kallipolis Ave. 43, Lykavitos. **Antonakis Tavern,** Germanou Patron St. 18, tel. 464697. **Cellari,** Korai St. 17, tel. 431099, guitar music and Greek songs. **Mikis Night Spot,** International Fair Highway, tel. 353925.

🏛 **Cyprus Museum,** the island's most important archaeological museum, Museum St., tel. 302189. Open Monday through Saturday 9 am-5 pm, Sunday 10 am-1 pm. **Byzantine Museum and Icon Museum,** Archbishop Makarios III Cultural Foundation, Arch. Kyprianou Square, tel. 456781, open Mon-Fri 9 am-4:30 pm, Sat 9 am-1 pm. **House of Hadji Georgakis Kornesios,** Patriarch Gregorios St., open Mon-Fri 8 am-2 pm, Sat 9 am-1 pm. **Jewelry Museum,** Praxippos St. 7-9, Laiki Yitonia, open Mon-Fri 10 am-4:30 pm. **Ayios Ioannis Cathedral,** Arch. Kyprianos Square, open Mon-Sat 8 am-12 pm and 2-4 pm. **Leventis Municipal Museum,** Hippokrates St., tel. 451475, open Tue-Sun 10 am-4:30 pm. **National Struggle Museum,** Arch. Kyprianos Square, tel. 302465, open Mon-Fri 8 am-2:30 pm and 3-6 pm. **Omeriye Mosque,** Tyllirias Square,open Mon-Sat 10 am-12:30 pm and 1:30-3:30 pm. **Municipal Art Gallery/Municipal Arts Center,** Apostle Barnabas St. 19, open Tue-Sat 10 am-3 pm and 5-11 pm, Sun 10 am-4 pm. **Municipal Cultural Center in the Famagusta Gate,** Nikiphoros Phokas Ave., open Mon-Fri 9 am-1 pm and 4-7 pm. **Folk Art Museum,** within the Archbishopric, Arch. Kyprianos Square, tel. 463205, open Mon-Fri 9 am-5 pm, Sat 10 am-1 pm.

📷 **Late June/Early July:** *Cyprus Music Days,* week-long music festival with numerous big-name artists from all over the world, jazz or classical music every other year (2001: Jazz). **End of September:** *Cyprus Rally,* three-day car race with international participants, with points toward the European Championship. Starts and finishes in Nicosia. **October 1:** *Cyprus Independence Day,* military parade at 11 am and public reception in the Presidential Palace in the evening.

🖼 *ART GALLERIES:* **Apokalypse,** corner of Avlonos St./Chytron St., tel. 766655. **Argo,** Dighenis Akritas Ave. 64E, tel. 754009. **Gloria,** Sozos St. 3A, tel. 762605. **Opus 39,** Kimonos St. 21, tel. 424983. *THEATER:* **ENA,** Athens St. 4, tel. 348203. **Municipal Theatre,** Museum St., tel. 463028. **Satyrico,** Vl. Kafkarides Cultural Centre, tel. 421609. *CITY SIGHTSEEING TOURS*: The Tourist Office organizes a twice-weekly two-hour tour of the Old Town from their bureau in Laiki Yitonia, Tuesdays and Thursdays at 10 am.

➕ **Emergency:** For police and ambulance dial: 199. **Hospital:** Nicosia General Hospital, Homer Ave., tel. 451111 and 452760.

✉ **Post Office** at Eleftheria Square, open Mon-Fri 7:30 am-2:30 pm, Thursdays also 3:15-6 pm.

🚌 *BUSES / SERVICE (GROUP) TAXIS:* **Kemek Transport** runs buses to other towns from 34 Leonidas St., tel. 463989. **Kyriakos Taxis** run mini-buses and service taxis to Limassol, Paphos and Larnaka from 27 Stassinos Ave., tel. 444141. Service taxis run daily 6 am to 6 pm (until 7 pm in summer). **Karydas,** Homer Ave. 8, tel. 462269. **Kypros,** Stassinos Ave. 9, tel. 464811. **Makris,** Stassinos Ave. 114, tel. 466201. *RENTAL CARS:* **Andy Spyrou/Europcar,** Armenias St. 11, tel. 338226, fax 338227. **Ansa,** Eleftherias Square, tel. 472352, fax 311293. **Carop,** Eleftherias Square, tel. 472333, fax 311293. **Hertz,** Metochiou St. 66A, Enkomi, tel. 477411, fax 461428. **Petsas & Sons,** Pantelidis Ave. 24A, tel. 462650, fax 366002.

🛍 Lefkara lace, hand-woven tablecloths and pillow cases as well as silverware, copperware and pottery can be found in the shops on Ledra Street and the adjoining streets or in the **Cyprus Handicrafts Service Shops** (Athalassa Ave. 186, tel. 305024 and Aristokypou St. 6 in Laiki Yitonia, tel. 303065). Many shops in Nicosia are closed for a week or ten days around August 15.

Detailed travel literature on Cyprus can be found in the **MAM** bookstore in Laiki Gitona, open Mon, Tue, Thur and Fri from 8 am-1 pm and 4-7 pm, Wed and Sat 8 am-3 pm.

TROODOS REGION (☎ 02)

KAKOPETRIA

🛏 😊😊😊 **Linos,** in the historic town center, tel. 923161, fax 923181, traditionally furnished rooms in a restored natural stone house (under preservation order). Some of the bathrooms have a whirlpool. 😊😊 **Hellas,** Mammantos St. 4, tel. 922450, fax 922227. **Makris Sunotel,** Mammantos St. 48, tel. 922419, fax 923367. 😊 **Hekali,** Grivas Dighenis St. 22, tel. 922501, fax 922503. **Krystal,** Grivas Dighenis St. 15, tel. 922433.

KALOPANAYIOTIS

🛏 😊 **Heliopolis,** tel. 952451. **Kastalia,** tel. 952455, fax 351288. **Loutraki,** tel. 952356.

PEDHOULAS

🛏 😊😊 **The Churchill Pinewood Valley,** tel. 952211, fax 952439. **Jack's,** tel. 952350, fax 952817, highly recommended, friendly, clean and comfortable.

MYTHOLOGY AND LITERATURE

Cyprus is for romantics. Lore and poetry abound, much of it about Aphrodite, whom Sappho called the "Queen of Cyprus." The Cypriots have their own epic poet, Stassinos, and Shakespeare's *Othello* is also set on this island. The revered Greek poet Georgios Seferis combined ancient references with local settings in poetry he composed on Cyprus.

The Golden Goddess

The birth of Aphrodite from the sea is lyrically described by an anonymous poet in the second *Homeric Hymn to Aphrodite* (Charles Boer, translator):

... beautiful Aphrodite...
the damp force
of Zephyros breathing
carried her along
on waves of the resounding sea
in soft foam.
In their own fillets of gold
the Horae received her happily,
and happily put
the ambrosial garments
around her.
On her immortal head
they placed a crown
that was carefully made,
beautiful and in gold.
On her silver-white breasts
they arranged necklaces of gold,
which they made themselves.

Adorned in this fashion, the newborn goddess was led to the gods. They reached out their hands to this smiling beauty crowned in violets, were awed by her and desired her as their bride.

The poet of this hymn does not mention the mutilation and gore of her conception as Hesiod does in his *Theogony*:

Preceding pages and right: Petra tou Romiou - the origin of the seductress Aphrodite. Here, the goddess borne of the sea is said to first have stepped ashore.

When father Uranus (Sky) held back the delivery of Mother Gaia's (Earth) offspring, she cried out for relief and revenge, and son Cronos came to her rescue. He hacked off his father's genitals and hurled them into the sea. From the semen, blood and sea foam Aphrodite was born, the only deity of her generation not born of Mother Earth. First she drifted near the island of Kythera (Cerigo), then to Cyprus, where she rose out of the sea. And wherever she went, "flowers grew where she stepped".

Aphrodite's birth was a synthesis of sheer opposites, for out of violence and ugliness the bearer of love and beauty was born. The gods themselves were seduced by her grace and erotic nature, this goddess who unites humans in love and joy, and fosters social graces and harmony.

On Cyprus, she was identified with the Phoenician fertility goddess Astarte and the divine Ishtar. According to Karl Kerenyi in *Goddesses of Sun and Moon*, she is a symbol of wholeness and union, and an amalgamation of opposites. To Jungians, she represents the synthesizing aspect of the psyche, a fusion of male-female attributes, as personified by Hermaphrodite, the offspring of Hermes and Aphrodite. The so-called Aphroditos is a bearded goddess representing the hermaphroditic form, and others have been found at Aphrodite's shrines such as Amathus.

One can see the very place where Aphrodite was born at Petra tou Romiou, a large rock in the sea near Palea Paphos. From here she emerged annually with renewed virginity, according to Robert Ranke-Graves in *The White Goddess*.

Aphrodite is said to be a bringer of harmony and joy. Yet she also brings calm, for her birth is said to have stilled the stormy seas. However, she also caused her share of trouble. Her innocence lacks any conscience and she can often lie and disregard reason. Artemis, Athena and

Hestia disliked her ways, not surprising considering they represented virginity and domesticity. Aphrodite's unromantic husband Hephaestus had his problems when she bedded down with the war god Aries. Helen said she was powerless against Aphrodite, using this as an excuse for yielding to Paris, which resulted in the Trojan War, which lasted ten years.

Despite her bad reputation, Aphrodite reigned supreme on Cyprus. She was worshiped at numerous shrines and among her epithets used by outsiders were "Lady of Paphos" and "Cyprian," the latter which came to have a lewd connotation. On Cyprus, however, she was often simply referred to as "The Goddess" or "The Lady," and her surname, if used, was *Eleamon*, meaning "The Merciful." An oiled stone and conical omphalos stones are most likely representations of the goddess. Until recently, new mothers prayed to these sacred objects. Other evidence exists to attest to the continuation of the influence of Aphrodite.

At the end of the Mycenaean Era in the late 12th century B.C., temples were built to other gods also. Apollo and Zeus became very important, though they did not displace this goddess of the sea. One is tempted to say that of all the gods Aphrodite came closest to expressing the nature of the inhabitants of Cyprus, being both joyful and sensual.

Tradition has set the location of Aphrodite's temple at Palea Paphos. Legend tells of different founders, including Kinyras, King of Paphos. According to the *Iliad*, this priest-king got into trouble for tricking Agamemnon, commander at Troy. After promising to send 50 ships to Troy, Kinyras sent one real ship and 49 models. Angry Agamemnon captured the island and drove him out. Kinyras eventually met his death as the penalty for losing a musical contest to Apollo.

Other members of the Kinyras' family also suffered for their father's deception. Aphrodite caused his three daughters to sleep with strangers. The fourth, Smyrna (or Myrra) who claimed to be more beau-

tiful than the goddess, was driven to incest with King Kinyras.

Adonis and Aphrodite

Christian celebrations of springtime rebirth appear to descend from pagan practices. Of the several versions of the story of Adonis and Aphrodite, the following is the traditional one: Adonis was born of an incestuous union between King Kinyras and his daughter Myrra. Myrra was later turned into a myrtle tree for the sin she had committed. When the trunk of this myrtle trunk was split, baby Adonis was found inside.

Aphrodite loved him right from the beginning, from infancy, and sent him to Persephone of the underworld to be taken care of for part of each year. But her many warnings against hunting large game

Above: Marble statues in the Cyprus Museum in Nicosia, centering around Aphrodite. Right: Nobel Prize winner for literature, Georgios Seferis (1900-1971).

were ignored, and he was killed whilst hunting a wild boar. Grieving Aphrodite caused the red anemones of springtime to blossom from Adonis' blood. Cult rituals celebrating the annual rebirth of Adonis included the planting of spring flowers.

In the book *Cyprus, a Portrait and Appreciation* by Sir Harry Luke, the pagan celebration of the return of spring is connected with a celebration at Larnaca, re-enacting the raising of Lazarus from the dead. Each year on the Sunday preceding Palm Sunday, a boy is draped in burial shrouds and laid out on a bed of flowers. When the priest pronounces, "Lazarus, come forth", the boy rises in joy. In another local celebration, Lazarus drifts ashore by boat amid splashing that recalls the playful bathing of Aphrodite's virgins.

Cyprus' Epic Poet

Cyprus had its own Homer in the author of a lost epic entitled *Cypria*. It is a set of stories about events that precede the action of Homer's *Iliad*, but only a paraphrased version of the epic survives. The author, Stassinos, is said to have been a son-in-law of Homer. Events leading up to the Trojan War are covered, including Zeus' plan to wipe out all evil, the beauty contest that sets off the conflict when Aphrodite bribes Paris by offering him Helen, the rounding up of reluctant generals, Achilles at Skyros, the deserting of Philoktetes on Lemnos, and many more.

The Roots of Othello

The story of the ill-fated love affair between Othello and Desdemona, a romance which was set on Cyprus, is the basis of Shakespeare's tragic play *Othello*. Shakespeare's source is Giraldi Cintio's 16th century Italian novel about a virtuous Venetian beauty named Desdemona who fell in love with a valiant dark-skinned officer in the service of Venice and married him against her parents' wishes. She accompanied him to his new command post in Famagusta.

The bare plots spun by Shakespeare and Cintio are very similar. The evil machinations of an ensign (Shakespeare's Iago) play on Othello's naïveté and raise jealous passions leading to innocent Desdemona's murder. Motives, Othello's character, and consequences differ, however. Cintio has Othello and Iago both beat Desdemona to death and then have the house torn down upon her. And Othello undergoes a drawn-out punishment for this. From this basic story, Shakespeare formed a powerful personal tragedy by making honest Othello far too noble to suspect Iago of duplicity. He is so appalled by his terrible crime of suffocating his love, the epitome of goodness, that he can't allow himself to live.

Two possible candidates for the "real" Othello are Christoforo Moro, a Venetian lieutenant-governor of Cyprus, and Francesco de Sessa, an Italian soldier, the latter for his Moorishly dark complexion

and his long imprisonment on unnamed charges.

Georgios Seferis in Cyprus

Georgios Seferis, beloved Greek poet and 1963 Nobel Prize winner, lived and wrote on Cyprus until 1953. He dedicated his *Logbook III,* a collection of poems from that period, "To the People of Cyprus, in Memory and Love..." Most of his poems have Cyprus as their setting and many allude to both history and mythology. Seferis often gazed at photographs of local Cypriot scenes for inspiration as he wrote. His poem *Helena* is set in Platres, a lovely wooded village on a slope of the Troodos range. It is based on Euripides' play of the same name, in which a phantom resembling Helen was sent to Troy while the real Helen stayed in Egypt. The line "The nightingales won't let you sleep in Platres" is apt, as listening to their melancholy song in the springtime leads one to ponder on wars fought for false causes.

KOPIASTE : CYPRIOT CUISINE

One of the joys of visiting Cyprus is its eclectic cuisine, a tasty assortment of tidbits known as *meze*, or *mezedhes* in the plural, which can be eaten as starters, or a number of plates can be shared by those present to make a whole meal. Cypriot food incorporates influences from the Mediterranean and Middle East, resulting in a wide range of culinary treats.

Kopiaste means "Come and join us." You will often have this sentiment expressed to you, perhaps out in the country by shepherds eating a simple meal of cheese, olive oil and bread, or by a gathering of city dwellers sharing a sumptuous feast. In either case, the invitation is heartfelt and you will be made welcome if you accept. But be prepared to devote some time to the gastronomic adventure.

Above: An assortment of delicious Cypriot tidbits, known as "mezedhes" (meze). Right: A fisherman softening squid by beating them on rocks.

Cypriots regard dining out as a sensual, leisurely experience that can last for hours. They ascribe to the Mediterranean belief that it is detrimental to drink on an empty stomach, so it is not customary to drink without nibbling on some snacks. Meals tend to be later than in northern countries: lunch usually starts between 1 and 2 pm and dinner between 8 and 9 pm, or even later in summertime.

Cypriot dishes call for fresh ingredients and the main fat used is olive oil. Garlic, another essential in Cypriot cuisine, has been used for thousands of years. *Mezedhes* that use garlic include *skordhalia*, garlic bread sauce used for boiled vegetables and fish filets, especially codfish; *melintzanosalata*, eggplant dip served cold with bread; and *tahini*, sesame dip with lemon juice and parsley, originating in the Middle East.

Houmous, a dip combining sesame paste and chickpeas, is another Middle Eastern favorite. Sesame seeds, grown in Cyprus up to 600 meters above sea level, are used in many dishes and breads. They are high in protein, calcium and lecithin, and contain vitamins C, E and some B complex. Sesame is also used for the rich sweet *halva* blended together with pistachio nuts. In Paphos, a number of different pies with meat or egg inside are made with sesame-sprinkled dough.

Talatouri, a dip made from yoghurt, garlic and cucumber and accented with dried mint, is a variation of *tzatziki* found on mainland Greece and in Turkey.

Cypriots are creative with spicy meat concoctions, the best known being *sheftalia*, grilled rolls of pork and beef sausage served as a warm *meze* or main course. *Lountza* is a distinctive Cypriot specialty of smoked filet of pork soaked in red wine, sprinkled with fresh coriander and sun-dried for a couple of days.

Hiromeri is another traditional dish of smoked ham marinated in wine. It is served cold, often with melon in the summer, or fried, quite tasty in omelets.

Pastourma is an Armenian specialty, a Middle Eastern *pastrami*. Once made of camel meat, it now consists of spicy beef and garlic, hung to dry for several days. *Aphelia* are pork spareribs marinated in red wine.

Gourounopoulo, or tender oven-baked suckling pig, is a favorite festive dish and often the forte of a master chef.

Game dishes include thrush in wine sauce, duck or turkey casseroles, and oven-baked partridges.

Strangely enough, fish is not abundant on Cyprus, but the Paphos District has the best supply, including *barbouni* (red mullet), *ksiphias* (swordfish) and *maridhes* (whitebait). Also, the fresh trout, *pestropha,* from the Troodos farms is very delicious.

Pastries stuffed with meat or vegetables are an island tradition. Bourekia, scalloped fan-shaped pastry stuffed with minced meat or cheese, constitute filling hot *mezedhes*.

A unique Cypriot specialty is *kolokotes*, which is a pastry stuffed with pumpkin, crushed wheat, raisins and sometimes pine nuts. It is, without doubt, an absolutely delectable dish that is healthy as well.

The most notable soup is *trahanas*, a Cypriot staple made from crushed wheat dried with yoghurt (*trahanas*), cooked in chicken broth and served with *haloumi*, sheep's milk cheese. *Haloumi* is also served alone as a *meze*, when it is usually fried or cooked on charcoal. A by-product of it is *anari*, the delicious bland condensed whey, which is best served warm. One delightful use of *anari* is in *bourekia tis anaris*, a pastry filled with the creamy cheese. Yoghurt, still made locally especially in Troodos, is a creamy, slightly sweet item resembling cottage cheese.

Vegetables are almost always simmered in casseroles; full of flavor but not crispy. *Imam Bayildi*, a Turkish dish, is an eggplant casserole with tomato sauce,

garlic and onions. Tomatoes or zucchini stuffed with rice, spices and cheese are reliable standards. *Kolokassi Mesaritiko* is a typical Cypriot recipe for *kolokassi*, a strange-looking vegetable root similar to a sweet potato that is cooked in a casserole with celery, onions and wine.

Gliko are any and every type of fruit (or vegetable) preserved in honey and served in every home, with a glass of water, to guests. It is too cloyingly sweet for many palates, but it is an obligatory social gesture to go through the motions of appreciation while eating it (and hope you won't be offered more!). *Shiamali* are semolina cakes subtly accented by rose water, almonds and yoghurt. *Loukmadhes* are little balls of dough fried and dipped in syrup. *Soutzoukos* is a solidified grape juice sweet made with almonds and formed into sausage-like rolls.

Common Menu Items

Soups: *Avgolemeno*: Chicken soup with egg-lemon sauce. *Patcha*: Sheep's

brains and innards in broth. *Psarosoupa*: Fish soup.

Mezedhes: *Taramasalata*: Pink fish roe salad. *Koupepia* or *dolmadhes*: Vine leaves stuffed with rice and meat.

Main Dishes: *Keftedhes*: Meatballs. *Klephtiko*: Lamb roasted in a sealed earthenware pot. *Moussaka*: Layered eggplant and potatoes with minced meat topped by bechamel sauce. *Souvlaki*: Lamb or pork kebab cooked on a spit. *Stiphado*: Veal or beef cooked in a casserole with onions. *Tavas*: Lamb casserole cooked in a sealed earthenware pot. *Yiouvetsi*: Casserole of lamb and pasta.

Fish and Seafood: *Bakalalarios*: Cod. *Garidhes*: Shrimp. *Melanouri*: Local panfish with a black spot on the tail.

Salads: *Khoriatiki*: A village salad, like Greek. *Khorta*: Steamed vegetables.

Vegetables: *Anginares*: Artichokes. *Bamies*: Okra. *Fasolia*: Green beans. *Kolokithakia*: Zucchini. *Koukia*: Broad beans. *Louvia*: Black-eyed peas. *Maroulia*: Lettuce. *Pantzaria*: Beets. *Patates*: Potatoes. *Spanaki*: Spinach.

Sweets: *Baklava*: Filo pastry filled with ground walnuts and sometimes pistachios with a fine honey-lemon sauce.

Fruit: *Karpouzi*: Watermelon. *Kerasia*: Cherries. *Mespila*: Loquats. *Papoutsosika*: Prickly pears. *Peponi*: melon. *Rodhia*: Pomegranate (the red juice of which is sometimes served ice-cold). *Sika*: Figs.

A Few Words about Coffee

If you ask for a Greek coffee (which is the same as Turkish coffee), you will get *kafe* - a potent brew served together with the grounds in tiny cups. If you would like it without sugar, ask for *sketo*, with a little sugar *metrio* and with a lot of sugar *gliko*.

Nescafé is found almost everywhere and, occasionally, filtered (sometimes called French) coffee as well. Very refreshing is *frappé*, drunk cold.

Above: Soutzoukos, a solidified grape juice sweet with almonds, a Cypriot speciality.

CYPRIOT WINE

Cyprus is considered one of the first countries in which grapes were harvested and wine was produced. The earliest known reference to Cypriot wine is from a playful painting circa 900 B.C. on the so-called Hubbard Amphora. According to the dramatist Euripides, the ancients referred to wine as Cypriot *Nama,* which in the era of Christianity meant the "Wine of the Holy Eucharist," showing the reverence in which they held it. Allegedly when Mark Antony presented Cyprus to Cleopatra he gallantly said, "Your sweetness, my love, is equal to that of Cyprus Nama." During the Classical Age, a society flourished with its prosperity based on the growing of grapes, wine production and trade.

Many mosaics, drawings and sculptures from this period indicate the importance of wine in daily life. A chalice dating from the sixth century B.C. found at the ancient city of Marion, close to modern Polis, has an inscription which says "Be happy and drink well."

Many writers, from ancient times until the present, have commented on Cypriot wine. It was praised by Homer, the poet Pindarus and Roman writer Pliny, who considered Cypriot wine superior to all others in the world. When the Jews worshiped in the Temple of King Solomon, the High Priest's offerings included the famous wine of Cyprus *Yen Cafrissin.*

Many of the world-renowned wines are made from vines introduced into Europe from Cyprus after the Crusades. A charming tale traces the origin of Champagne to Cyprus. Early in the 1300s, Count Thibaut IV of Champagne was returning from a crusade and stopped on Cyprus. While there, a young noble of the Queen's court had been sentenced to death for sneaking into the royal apartments to visit his betrothed. Count Thibaut asked that his life be spared under the condition he take him along to Champagne. Once there, the young noble pined away for his love. Count Thibaut finally urged him to return to Cyprus, marry his sweetheart and return to Champagne. More than a year later, the Count was surprised when a visit was announced from the noble and his new bride. The happy couple presented gifts to Thibaut. The bride offered a rose bush, which became the fragrant rose of Provence. The noble brought cuttings from the best vines of Olympos, which, when planted on the chalky cliffs of the Marne, became Champagne.

During the period following Richard the Lionheart's conquest of the island in 1191, Cyprus' most famous wine, *Commandaria,* was made for the first time. The production of the legendary dessert wine was carried on in the commanderies of the Knights of St. John, which gave their name to the wine. The recipe for *Commandaria* wine was already described by Hesiod in 800 B.C. as "Leave the grapes ten days in the sun and then ten nights and then five days in shade and eight more in the jar." Young *Commandaria* wine is yellowish-white in hue, becoming a ruby-red color through aging. The grapes, grown above 900 meters in the villages of Zoopiyi, Kalokhorio and Ayios Konstantinos, are picked late in the season when they have fully developed their sweet flavor. Hesiod's recipe is still followed to this day, as the grapes are spread out in the sun for 14 days to concentrate their sugar content. The wine is kept in the *Commandaria* villages for two years and subsequently kept at least a year in a barrel in Limassol. Fully mature wine, called *Mana* (Greek for "mother"), remains in oak barrels until added to the immature wine, and is allowed to sit with it for seven years before it is sold. The oak barrels of the Mana never stand empty.

Another wine which was very popular during medieval times was *Malmsey.* The name is derived from the port of

Monemvasia in the Peloponnese, but it was made on Cyprus as well. The red *Malvoisie* grape still grows to this day on the slopes of the Troodos mountains.

Wine production was especially refined and cultivated during the reign of the Lusignans and later the Venetians. It is said that it was the fine wines of Cyprus that led the Turkish Sultan Selim II (better known as Selim the Sot) to overrun the island in 1571. This marked the beginning of 300 years of Turkish occupation. Although there was a decline in the quality of wine produced on Cyprus during the Turkish Period, it remained the island's most important agricultural export product.

Some of the oldest wine on the island is privately bottled and sold on, and a particularly delightful local custom calls for burying a filled jar of wine near the house when a child is born. When the child marries, the jar is dug out and its contents are

Above: A vintner, proud of his produce, checks the color of his wine.

served, so many years later, to the guests at the wedding party.

A large percentage of Cypriot wines are produced in the island's four biggest wineries. The large cooperative SODAP, founded in 1947, owns two large wineries in Limassol and Paphos. Members and shareholders are all vinegrowers. ETKO, in Limassol, is the successor to the C. Hadjipavlou Company formed in 1844. LOEL is a public company formed by vinegrowers in 1943. KEO was formed as a private company in 1926, but today it belongs to the Hellenic Group of Mining Companies. The KEO enterprise owns four wineries, two of them are in the Troodos Mountains, one is in Paphos, and the main plant is headquartered in Limassol. As well as this, KEO (leaders in the export market) owns three experimental vineyards, and one of its many achievements is the introduction of new scientific methods in the wine industry. KEO introduced the first Cypriot sherry in the early 1930s and now also produces a good lager beer.

Sunshine is essential for the production of top-quality grapes, but not scorching heat, which weakens the acidity of the crop. The southern slopes of the Troodos Mountains as well as the high altitude villages in Limassol and Paphos offer perfect conditions for grape ripening.

Commandaria wine is made from the two most popular grape varieties, the largest portion from the *Mavro* red grape with the addition of the *Xynistri* white grape. Together with the *Maratheftiko* and *Ofthalmo*, two potent red varieties, they cover close to 100 square kilometers of the total 110 square kilometers under vine cultivation on Cyprus. Over 100 varieties of grapes are grown here. About 55 percent of the entire harvest are grown in the Paphos District, but Limassol is the chief wine-production and exporting center.

Newer white varieties that were introduced to Cyprus in the middle of the last century include the Iberian *Palomino* and *Malaga* grape; the Alsatian *Riesling* and the white *Lefkas*, from the Greek island of Lefkada. The prevalent *Cabernet Sauvignon*, black grapes imported from France and the black *Shiraz*, imported from Australia, have made big headway in popularity.

Here is a selection of some of the best labels to sample while visiting Cyprus:

Red Wines

Agravani (Ecological Winery of Ayios Amvrosios): Blend of *Cabernet*, *Carignan* and *Mataro*.

Semeli (ETKO): Blend of *Mavro* and imported varieties.

Kilani Village (Ayia Mavri): Estate-bottled *Xynistri*.

Peratis (Menagros Winery): Dry blend of *Mavro*, *Carignan Noir* and *Grenache*.

Plakota (Vouni-Panayia): Blend of *Mavro*, *Chiraz* and *Mavrotheftiko*. Distinguished by a characteristic aroma.

White Wines

Ayios Andronikos, Monte Royia (Khrysorroyiatissa Monastery), Cellar Antoine (KEO): Crisp dry wine of *Xynistri* grapes.

Kilani Village (Ayia Mavri): Blend mostly of *Mavro*.

Amathus (LOEL): Fragrant *Palomino* and others.

Ambelida (Ecological Winery of Ayios Amvrosios): Dry, light wine produced from *Xynistri*.

Cellar Arsinoe (SODAP): Well-balanced *Xynistri*.

Rosé Wines

Rosé wines are made from red grapes but the must is not fermented on the lees, in order to achieve a lighter color. The blending of white and red grapes to make rosé is forbidden.

Coeur de Lion (KEO), named for King Richard the Lionheart: Dry, light wine made from *Grenache Noir*.

Mirto (SODAP): Fine wine with pleasant aroma produced from *Mavro* grapes.

Pampela (Vouni-Panayia): Dry, light wine made from a blend of *Mavro*, *Ofthalmo* and *Lefkas*.

The major wineries all offer tours of their premises. A good time to sample different types of wine is at the eleven-day Limassol Wine Festival, taking place in late August/early September.

Poke around in local *cavas* (wine shops) to find unusual bottles of vintage standard. Wineries also make brandy, and some of the fruity ones are very tasty. *Brandy sour*, a cocktail correctly made with fresh lemon juice, is a big favorite in the summertime. Another by-product that separates the faint-hearted from the robust is *zivania* (Trester), a clear, deceptively innocent-looking spirit produced from grape mash, but upon sampling this firewater reveals its true spirit.

METRIC CONVERSION

Metric Unit	US Equivalent
Meter (m)	39.37 in.
Kilometer (km)	0.6241 mi.
Square Meter (sq m)	10.76 sq. ft.
Hectare (ha)	2.471 acres
Square Kilometer (sq km)	0.386 sq. mi.
Kilogram (kg)	2.2 lbs.
Liter (l)	1.05 qt.

TRAVEL PREPARATIONS

Climate / Travel Season

Cyprus has a Mediterranean climate, with long, dry summers from mid-May to mid-October and mild winters from December until February. In the spring, temperatures average between 12° and 20°C; in summer between 25° and 30°C. The warmest time of the year is July and August, when midday temperatures reach 40°C. The coolest period is January and February, when temperatures average between 10° and 11°C; they only rarely get as low as freezing and usually only in the mountainous areas.

Rainfall reaches about 300-400 mm per year and is heaviest in January and February, when snow often coats the Troodos peaks. The sun shines year round, with an average of six or seven hours of sunshine in January and February, and 12 or more in mid-summer. It is possible to swim any time of the year with the exception of the coldest periods.

Clothing and Equipment

Experienced travelers generally like to travel light, bringing clothes they can wash out and dry in hotel rooms. Lightweight cotton clothing is recommended, along with sweaters and windbreaker jackets. Bring comfortable, sturdy boots for hiking, canvas shoes and sandals for strolling in towns. Cool shirts, cotton skirts, beach towels and sandals can easily be bought on the island, but bathing suits and cotton underwear is best bought at home. (Bathing suits are essential, as nude bathing is not recommended on Cyprus!) If you go in fall or winter, bring warm clothes and a light coat, as well as a travel umbrella.

Casual wear and sandals can be worn in the evening. For better restaurants or clubs, it is better to bring something more elegant. Do not forget that you will require suitably modest clothing if you want to enter churches.

Entry Requirements / Visas

Republic (South) of Cyprus: For a stay of up to 90 days you need a valid passport, but no visa is required for citizens of the U.S., Canada, Australia, New Zealand, EU or Switzerland. Children under 16 years of age must have a passport or be entered in the passport of the accompanying parent. Visitors may enter or exit only via the international airports of Larnaca and Paphos, or the sea ports of Larnaca and Limassol.

Northern Cyprus: Day trips from Nicosia across the Green Line into Turkish territory are usually permitted by the Cyprus Government. Details are not available by phone. Should you require more details, you will have to go to the Ledra Palace Checkpoint. You can only cross the Green Line between 8 am and midday, on foot (the journey can be continued by taxi on the other side). After passport control in the Republic, you cross the UN buffer zone to the adjacent border control, where you are provided with a day visa and told the precise time of your return that evening. Your passport is not stamped, and you must make sure to return not later than the time stated, or the Republic may well deny you re-entry. You should not make any purchases in Northern Cyprus, as they may be confiscated if found.

Vaccinations are not required, but having a tetanus shot before traveling is recommended.

Currency / Foreign Exchange

The Cyprus Pound (C£) is divided into 100 cents. Notes are in 5, 10 and 20 pound denominations; coins in 1, 2, 5, 10, 20 and 50 cent (c) denominations. One C£ = US $1.87 / UK £1.15.

Eurochecks, traveler's checks and credit cards are accepted, though not all cards by all banks. There are exchange services at all the airports and ports. There is no limit to the amount of currency you may bring in. Amounts in excess of the equivalent of US $1,000 must be declared on arrival, if you plan to take more than that amount back out of the country when you leave.

Customs and Import Regulations

Visitors may import articles for personal use without payment of duty. The follow articles may also be imported, free of duty: 200 cigarettes or 50 cigars or 250 grams of tobacco; 1 liter of spirits; 0.75 liter of wine; 0.30 liter of perfume; other articles (except jewelry) up to a total value of C£50.

There is not much point in attempting to bring a pet along on your holiday: animals must be quarantined for six months upon arrival.

Warning: The export of antiquities without prior permission and without having received a licence from the Department of Antiquities is absolutely forbidden and could result in arrest and time in prison!

Motor vehicles, trailers and boats can be imported toll-free for a period of up to three months. For further information, regulations and advice regarding bringing a motor vehicle to Cyprus, contact the *Cyprus Automobile Association*, 12 Chr. Mylonas St., P.O. Box 22279., CY-2014 Nicosia, tel. (02) 313233, fax. 313482.

An international or national driver's license and certificate of registration are required. Green card insurance is not accepted or valid in Cyprus. Visitors are obliged to take out a short-term insurance policy with one of the companies on the island.

GETTING THERE

By Plane

More than 30 airlines connect Cyprus with major European and Middle Eastern cities. Cyprus Airways flies from and to Athens, London, Gatwick, Birmingham, Manchester, Paris, Berlin, Munich, Frankfurt, Zurich, Geneva, Tel Aviv, Jeddah, Dubai, Riyadh, Bahrain, Kuwait, Dhahran, Cairo and Damascus, among other cities.

Cyprus Airways: Nicosia, 21 Alkeus St., P.O. Box 21903, tel. (02) 663054. Ticketing Office: 50 Arch. Makarios III Ave., tel. (02) 751996. Branches of Cyprus Airways are also to be found in the town of Limassol, Larnaca, Paphos and Athens.

From Paphos airport an hourly bus service into the town is available. From Larnaca's airport there is no bus service into town, although private taxis offer their services round the clock. Both of the airports offer the following services: tourist information bureaus, foreign exchange, coin-operated telephones, car rental, hotel reservation assistance, facilities for the physically handicapped, duty-free shops, health inspector's office and several cafeterias. At the airport in Larnaka there is also a post and telegraph office.

By Ship

Passenger ships and car ferries connect Cyprus with Piraeus (Athens' harbor) and the island of Rhodes and also Iraklion on Crete. There are also connections to several Italian ports. An information brochure on ferry transportation to and from

Guidelines

the island can be obtained from the Cyprus Tourism Organization (CTO) offices in Cyprus and abroad.

Ferries from Piraeus to Limassol (and continuing to Haifa, if desired) run three times weekly. The total travel time is about 38 to 44 hours.

Shipping Companies:

Poseidon Lines: Piraeus, 32 Alkyondon Ave., tel. (01) 965-8300, fax (01) 965-8310; Limassol, 124 Roosevelt Ave., tel. (05) 745666, fax (05) 745577.

Salamis Lines: Piraeus, 9 Filellinon St., tel. (01) 429-4325, fax (01) 429-4557; Limassol, C. Hadjipavlos St., Salamis House, tel. (05) 355555, fax. (05) 364410.

TRAVELING IN CYPRUS

You can travel within Cyprus by bus, taxi, service (group) taxi or rented car. There are no trains or rail transport whatsoever on the island. Tours and sightseeing cruises are organized all year round by various tour operators.

By Bus and Taxi

Bus: Numerous bus companies operate between the towns and resorts. Urban buses run frequently during the day, but operate only until 7 pm in summer in tourist areas. Village buses make one run to the city each weekday, leaving the village early in the morning and returning in the afternoon. All major bus stations and connections are given in the *INFO* section of each travel chapter.

Service (Group) Taxis: This is a convenient and reasonable form of transportation between towns. Usually seven to ten persons share one large taxi. Passengers arrange in advance where they will be picked up and dropped off at the stop of their choice along the route. Make sure to make a return reservation at a specific hour and location, especially on weekends when most taxis are full. Your hotel or the local tourist office can help you

with schedules and reservations. Service taxis are frequent, reliable and cheaper than private taxis. But most service taxis make their last run at 7 pm, so bear this in mind when you plan your excursions within Cyprus. One service taxi company in each town operates on Sundays.

Private Taxis: Your hotel reception desk can call and have you picked up promptly. If you want a chauffeured excursion, agree on a price in advance. The charge is often based on time.

By Car

You drive on the left-hand side of the road in Cyprus. Main highways and city streets are in good condition. Some roads are only partially paved and lack hard shoulders, occasionally narrowing to a single lane. Some mountain roads are only narrow dirt lanes. Drive slowly and watch out for other vehicles, animals and pedestrians.

Distances and speed limits are posted in kilometers, and road signs are in English as well as Greek. The speed limit on main highways is 100 kmh and 80 kmh outside towns, 50 kmh in settled areas. Use of seat belts by front seat passengers is compulsory. Children over five may occupy the front passenger's seat if it is equipped with a child's safety belt.

You are legally drunk if your blood alcohol level is 0.9 per mill or higher.

By Rental Car

There are numerous rental agencies in the towns; the Cyprus Tourism Organization publishes a list of them. A valid international driver's license or license of one's country is required, as well as a minimum age of 21 years. The driver sits on the right, British style, with the gearshift to the left. The car is generally delivered to the driver with a full tank of gas, but the gas must be paid for at the time of pickup. However, if there is still gas in the tank when you return the car, you are not compensated for it! By prior arrangement, a car may be picked up at one place and delivered back to another.

Before setting out on a longer excursion, take the car on a test drive with someone from the agency to make sure it is working suitably. Don't underestimate the difficulty of switching to the British system if you are unfamiliar with it.

Hitchhiking

Hitchhiking is not forbidden in Cyprus but one must use good sense when doing so, as is true anywhere else. Generally, it is best for female hitchhikers to pair up with someone else, preferably a male, and to restrict the activity to the daytime. Cypriots are generally hospitable and will often pick up hitchhikers. It can be a lovely way to meet the locals while out in the mountains or countryside, and will spare you from waiting for hours for one of the local buses.

By Ship

Cruises: One-day sightseeing cruises are organized from May to October. Details are available from local sightseeing tour operators. Itineraries: From Limassol Harbor to Lady's Mile Beach and back; from Paphos Harbor to Coral Bay and to the coast of Peyia; from Ayia Napa to Paralimni, Protaras and back; from Larnaca along the coast to Ayia Napa and back; from Polis along the Akamas coast.

Yachting: *Larnaca Marina*, tel. (04) 653110, fax (04) 624110. Weather-protected berthing for 450 yachts, 10 minutes from the town center. Services available at reasonable rates include: Water, electricity (240v / 50hz), telephone and fax, fuel (N. Pier), repair facilities, laundry, showers, lockers, duty-free shops, post boxes, stringent 24-hour security. Customs and immigration formalities can be cleared here. *Limassol Sheraton Pleasure Harbor*, P.O. Box 10064, tel. (05) 321100 ext. 3312, fax. (05) 329208. Protected by breakwater, ideal for sail and motor boats. 227 protected berths.

Services include water, electricity, telephone, television hookup, shuttle buses, water taxis, 24-hour security, shopping, a market, yacht repair and a customs office.

Organized Tours

Over 250 travel agencies operate on the island, many of which are IATA members (*International Air Transport Association*). Cyprus also has its own travel association, ACTA (*Association of Cyprus Travel Agents*), and issues a directory each year. ACTA, P.O. Box 22369, CY-1521 Nicosia, tel. (02) 666435, fax 667593.

Many travel agencies operate full or half-day tours within Cyprus to major sights, and a few offer evening outings to clubs featuring music and folk dances.

Some reliable agencies are:
LIMASSOL: **A.L. Mantovani & Sons Ltd.** (American Express Agent), 1 Archbishop Kyprianous St., Loukiades Building, tel. (05) 362045, fax (05) 377842. *NICOSIA:* **Amathus Travel Ltd.**, 17 Homer Ave., tel. (02) 462101, fax (02) 451329. *POLIS:* **Century 21 Travel Agency**, Aphrodite St., tel. (06) 321658, fax (06) 321693. *PAPHOS:* **Exalt Tours**, 24 Agias Kyriakis St., tel. (06) 243803, fax (06) 246167. *LARNACA:* **Iason Tours,** Stratigos Timagia Ave., tel. (03) 636499, fax. (03) 821988.

PRACTICAL TIPS FROM A TO Z

Accommodation

Hotels in Cyprus are modern, and few are without air conditioning or private bathrooms. The *Cyprus Hotels Guide* printed by the Cyprus Tourism Organization lists almost all hotels, guest houses, B & B's and campsites, classifying hotels by the star system (*****) and apartment hotels according to categories (A to C). The guide also gives price ranges and telephone numbers. It is strongly recom-

Guidelines

mended to reserve summer accommodation in beach communities before arrival, and all year round in Nicosia. Most hotels offer discounts during the low season (November 16 to March 15), and Cyprus' mild climate makes it suitable for winter vacations.

Upon arrival at your hotel, clarify the terms of your accommodation (bed and breakfast, half-board, etc.). A charge of 50 percent of the daily rate is added to a bill if guests vacate the room after noon but before 6 pm.

The hotel categories in this book are to be interpreted as follows:

⊚ up to about 40 US dollars

⊚⊚ between 40 and 80 US dollars

⊚⊚⊚ from 80 US dollars (prices per double room not including breakfast).

Agrotourism: This is a favorite form of country accommodation in many Mediterranian countries, and is available on Cyprus. Numerous country houses in particularly beautiful settings are available for rent. Information and reservations through the CTO.

Camping is legally restricted to authorized campsites licensed by the CTO. Facilities include showers, toilets, minimarkets, small restaurants, and washing facilities. Electricity is charged as an extra.

LIMASSOL: **Governor's Beach Campsite**, tel. (05) 632300. 20 kilometers east of Limassol. Capacity for 111 caravans, 247 tents. Open year round.

PAPHOS: **Yeroskipou Zenon Gardens Camping**, tel. (06) 242277. 3 kilometers from Paphos. Capacity for 95 tents/caravans. Open April to October; **Feggari Camping**, Coral Bay, 11 kilometers north of Paphos, tel. (06) 621534. Open year round.

POLIS: **Polis Camping**, tel. (06) 321526. 500 meters from Polis in a eucalyptus grove by the beach. Capacity for 200 tents / caravans. Open March to October.

AYIA NAPA: **Ayia Napa Camping Site**, tel. (03) 721946. Near the beach. Capacity for 150 tents/caravans. Open March to October.

TROODOS MOUNTAINS: **Troodos Camping Site**, tel. (05) 421624. 2 kilometers from Troodos Hill Resort, off the main Troodos-Kakopetria road. Open May to October.

Electricity

Electricity is 240 volts. Three-pronged plugs are generally required for electrical appliances; adaptors are available at hotels and shops.

Festivals and Holidays

Official holidays: *New Year:* presents are exchanged among family and friends. *January 6: Epiphany,* blessing of the waters. Variable, 50 days before Easter: *Shrove Monday.* March 25: *Greek National Day* (Independence Day). April 1: *EOKA Day (Cypriot National Holiday).* Variable: *Greek Orthodox Easter Festival.* May 1: *Labor Day.* August 15: *Assumption Day.* October 1: *Independence Day.* October 28: *Greek-Cypriot National Day (Oxi Day,* commemorating the Greek Army's resistance to the Italians in 1940). December 24 (half-day). December 25/26: *Christmas.* December 31 (half-day).

As well as these national holidays, there are local and religious celebrations. One is *Kataklysmos,* celebrated mainly at Larnaca (with a large street fair) and other seaside towns, starting 50 days after Easter. Everyone joins in the fun and splashes their friends with sea water. The ritual is said to commemorate Lazarus. *St. Paul's Feast* is celebrated at Paphos on June 28 and 29. In summer, plays are performances at the ancient sites of Kourion and Paphos, and operas take place in Paphos Harbor.

Opening Hours

Banks: Mon-Fri 7:30 am to 2:30 pm (in Sept and June also Thur 3 to 6 pm).

Shops: Nov-March: Mon-Sat 9:30 am

to 6 pm, April/May and October until 7 pm and from June-Sept until 7:30 pm. Some shops close from 1 to 4 pm.

Museums: On holidays most museums and archaeological sites remain open, from 9 am to 5 pm. However, they are closed on Greek Easter Sunday. See info sections for opening times.

Post Offices: Mon-Sat 7:30 am to 1:30 pm, Thursdays also 3-6 pm. The following are open in the afternoons: *Nicosia*: Eleftheria Square. *Limassol*: Gladstone St. 1. *Larnaka*: King Paul Square. *Paphos*: Thermidos St./St. Paul St. Passports required for poste restante.

Press

The English-language daily newspaper is *The Cyprus Mail*. A lively and informative weekly newspaper is *The Cyprus Weekly. Time Out* is an entertainment and information guide. *Sunjet* is Cyprus Airways' interesting in-flight magazine.

Radio and Television

The Cypriot television channel Cyprus Broadcasting Television Station (CyBC) and the *Cyprus Broadcasting Corporation* radio station give news and weather forecasts in English each evening on Channel 2 (or 603 KHz or AM 498).

Socializing

Cypriots are gregarious people and love to socialize and also adore children. If you are invited to a Cypriot's home for dinner, a party or a wedding, make sure to accept! You can really get an insight into the culture this way. Almost all Cypriots understand some English, so you will easily find a number of people with whom you can converse. Social customs call for bringing a gift of some sort when visiting a Cypriot household. Flowers, a bottle of wine or sweets are appropriate.

Cypriots celebrate Name Days or the Saint's Day after whom they have been named, rather than birthdays. On the days of the most popular saints, such as Maria

on August 15 or Andreas (the most popular man's name on Cyprus) on November 30, family and close friends come calling. The honored person offers food and wine in a continual open house. If you are invited to stop by but cannot do so, you should at least call to extend your greetings.

Cypriot hospitality is legendary, so give up any notions of going "Dutch." Accept the generous gesture graciously with a smile!

Sports

Bowling: Nicosia: *Kykko Bowling,* near the Ledra Hotel, 5 kilometers from the town center. Limassol: *Limassol Bowling:* In the hotel area, east of the city center.

Cycling: Bikes can be rented in towns and resorts. Races in spring and fall are organized by *The Cyprus Cycling Federation*, P.O. Box 24572, CY 2406 Nicosia, tel./fax (02) 663344.

Diving: Spear fishing is prohibited in resort area marked with red buoys. For spear fishing with scuba gear a special license is required. Warning: it is forbidden to take sponges and antiquities from the sea bed!

Fishing: No license is required for sea fishing. Thirteen reservoirs are stocked with freshwater fish: trout, perch, bream, catfish and other species. Anglers older than 12 must apply for a license at the District Fisheries Department. Some reservoirs observe a fishing season. For fishing and spear fishing licenses and regulations, contact the local area administration office or the *Head Office of Fisheries Dept.*, Aiolou 13, CY 1101 Nicosia, tel. (02) 807830, fax 775955.

Golf: There are three 18-hole golf courses. *Tsada Golf Club*, 8 kilometers north of Paphos, tel. (06) 642774, fax 642776. *Secret Valley Golf Club*, 18 kilometers east of Paphos and 49 kilometers west of Limassol at Petra tou Romiou, tel./fax same as for Tsada Golf Club.

Guidelines

Elias Golf Course, by Pareklissia near Limassol, tel. (05) 325000.

Hiking: Hiking excursions can be arranged by tour organizers. *Troodos Area:* Four marked nature trails (Atalante, Artemis, Kaledonian and Persephone Trails). *Akamas Area:* Two posted nature trails (Aphrodite Trail, Adonis Trail). *Cape Greco:* One half-hour shore walk around the cape. *Stavros-tis-Psokas Area:* Two marked trails in Paphos Forest.

Horseback Riding: *Lapatsa Sporting Center,* Dheftera, 11 kilometers southwest of Nicosia. tel. (02) 621201. *Elias Beach Hotel and Country Club,* Limassol-Nicosia Road, five minutes drive from hotel area, *Pareklissia Junction,* tel. (05) 325000. Both centers are open year round. Hours must be booked in advance.

Water Sports: Swimming is popular along the 620 kilometer long coast from May until November. Only the truly hardy swim year round. CTO public beaches offer changing cabins, parasols, chairs and lifeguards.

Paphos Public Beach, Yeroskipos, 3 km east of Paphos Harbor, tel. (06) 234525; *Dassoudi Public Beach,* 5 km east of Limassol city center, tel. (05) 322881; *Larnaca Public Beach,* 10 km east of Larnaca center, tel. (04) 621311.

Private watersports schools are literally lined-up side by side along the beaches. One can rent speed boats, water scooters, sailboats, windsurfing boards, canoes, pedal boats and paragliders.

Skiing: On Mount Olympos (Khionistra) from January to March. The *Cyprus Ski Club*, P.O. Box 22185, CY 1518 Nicosia, tel. (02) 365340, fax 369681, operates two pistes and four lifts, two on the north face and two in Sun Valley, which has a cafeteria and three restaurants. Equipment and toboggans for rent, instruction offered.

Tennis: *Field Club,* Egypt Ave., Nicosia center, tel. (02) 452041; *Eleon Tennis Club,* 3 Ploutarchou St., Enkomi near Nicosia, tel. (02) 449923; *Lapatsa Sporting Center,* Dheftera, 11 kilometers southwest of Nicosia. *Limassol Sporting Club*, 4 J. Zachariadou, west of Limassol center, tel. (05) 359818; *Famagusta Tennis Club,* 3 Mesaorias St., Famagusta center, tel. (05) 335952. *Larnaca Tennis Club,* 10 Kilkis St., Larnaca center, tel. (04) 656999. *Yeroskipos Tourist Beach,* 3 kilometers east of Paphos Harbor, tel. (06) 234525.

Telecommunications

Using the telephone here is uncomplicated. Operators speak English and directories are printed in Roman letters. Pay phones may be used for local and international calls. Calls may be made from the special telephone offices (CTA) or from public card phones; phone cards (costing 3.5 or 10 Cypriot pounds) can be bought in kiosks and in post offices. Expect hotels to add a surcharge to the basic rate. The main post office also has a telefax service for the public.

The country code for Cyprus is +357 (then the area code without the zero, and then the phone number).

Calls from the Republic to Northern Cyprus are only possible through the telephone center of the United Nations.

For directory assistance in Cyprus dial 192 for national numbers and 194 for international numbers.

Tipping

A 10 percent service charge is added to the bill in restaurants, but not all of this goes to the waiter. It is polite to leave up to five percent more. Service taxi drivers who handle luggage, and porters and hotel maids should be given a reasonable tip at the end of the stay.

Tour Guides

Private tour guides can be hired for half or full days. Contact the *Cyprus Tourist Guides Assoc.*, P.O. Box 24942, CY-1355 Nicosia, tel. (02) 765755, fax 766872.

ADDRESSES

Tourist Information

The Cyprus Tourism Organization (CTO) has several offices throughout the country. Their literature is available free and maps and booklets for special needs and interests are very useful. The **Cyprus Traveler's Handbook** is a useful guide for phone numbers of public services and recreational facilities.

Information: **CTO Head Office**, P.O. Box 24535, CY-1390 Nicosia, tel. (02) 337715 fax (02) 331644, e-mail: cto@cto.org.cy.

CTO offices for different regions are listed in the INFO section of the relevant chapters. CTO offices abroad: *U.K.:* 213 Regent Street, London W1, tel. (071) 734-9822, fax. (071) 2876534. *U.S.:* 13 East 40th St., New York, N.Y. 10016, tel. (212) 683-2800, fax. (212) 683-5282.

Cyprus on the Internet: The homepage for Cyprus' tourist board is www.cyprustourism.org.

LANGUAGE GUIDE

Greek

Greek is the first official language of the Republic of Cyprus. Radio news broadcasts are also given in English in the evening. Almost all Cypriots speak some English, but they are delighted if you know at least a few basic Greek words and expressions. The dialect of Cyprus is called Kypriaka. It contains ancient Greek words, as well as Turkish.

Some Remarks on Pronunciation

kh is pronounced as hard ch, as in Bach; ch pronounced ch as a throaty hiss.

Common Words and Phrases

good morning	*kaliméra*
good afternoon	*chérete*
good evening	*kalispéra*
good night	*kaliníchta*
hello (plural or polite)	*ya sas*
hello (singular, familiar)	*ya su*
goodbye	*addío*
please	*parakaló*
thank you	*ephcharistó*
yes / no	*ne / ochi*
excuse me	*signómi*
none	*kanéna*
no problem	*kanéna provlima*
okay	*endáxi*
How are you?	
plural or polite:	*ti kánete?*
singular, familiar:	*ti kánis?*
Fine, thanks.	*kalá, ephcharistó*
My name is...	*onomásome...*
Do you speak...?	*ezis miláte...?*
English	*angliká*
I don't understand	*then katalavéno*
I'd like...	*thélo...*
I'm happy	*chérome*
I'm hungry	*pináo*
I'm thirsty	*thipsó*
I'm lost	*chátika*
it's urgent	*íne épigon*
Where is...?	*pu íne...?*
I'm sick	*íme árrostos (fem. árrosti)*
Help!	*voidia!*
How much?	*póso?*
How many?	*pósa?*
How?	*pos?*
Where?	*pu?*
When?	*póte?*
What time?	*tí óra?*
What?	*tí?*
Who?	*piós?*
Why?	*yatí?*
Is there?	*ipárchi?*
there is...	*ipárchi...*
there isn't.	*then ipárchi*
Where is?	*pu íne?*
expensive	*akrivó*
cheap	*phtinó*
beautiful	*ómorpho*
ugly	*áschimo*
near	*kondá*
far	*makriá*
left	*aristerá*
right	*theksiá*
today	*símera*
tomorrow	*ávrio*

Guidelines

yesterday.	*chtés*
hour	*óra*
day	*méra*
week	*evdomáda*
month	*mínas*
cold / hot	*kríos zestós*
open / closed	*aniktós / klistós*
one half	*misó*
one	*éna*
two	*thío*
three	*tría*
four	*téssera*
five	*pénde*
six	*éxi*
seven	*ephtá*
eight	*okhtó*
nine	*enniá*
ten	*théka*
hundred	*ekató*
thousand	*chília*
million	*éna ekatomírio*
Monday	*dephtéra*
Tuesday	*trítí*
Wednesday	*tetárti*
Thursday	*pémpti*
Friday	*paraskeví*
Saturday	*sávvato*
Sunday	*kiriakí*

CYPRUS AT A GLANCE

Information given here refers to the **Republic of Cyprus**, the internationally recognized government of the island.

Capital: Nicosia.

Founded: August 16, 1960.

Flag: Map of the island in gold above two crossed olive branches on a white background.

Description: The third largest Mediterranean island, Cyprus has an area of 9,251 square kilometers. It is located in the Eastern Mediterranean 65 kilometers from Turkey, 95 kilometers from Syria, 380 kilometers from Egypt, and 386 kilometers from Rhodes. The highest peak is Khionistra (Mount Olympos) at 1,951 meters. The two main mountain ranges are the Kyrenia Mountains (Pentadaktylos Range) in the north and the Troodos Mountains in the south.

Government: A democratic presidential republic with a 56-member parliament elected for four years.

Population: The entire island has a population of 810,000; 164,000 living in the northern Turkish section. Nearly two thirds of Cypriots work in the service industry; five percent work in agriculture.

Religion: 77% of the entire population are Orthodox Greek, 19% follow Islam and 4% belong to another denomination.

Education: Since September 1992, the *University of Cyprus* has existed in Nicosia. It has a Turkology faculty.

Commerce and Industry: Agriculture, wine, copper and gypsum mining, manufacture of textiles, shoes, cement. Tourism is an important source of income.

Membership: Commonwealth, Council of Europe, EU Member State, OECD.

AUTHOR

Waldemar Weiss studied geography and German literature, and for the past two decades has been directing educational tours to the countries of the Mediterranean, Malta and Cyprus. The experiences he has gathered as a travel writer have been published.

PHOTOGRAPHERS

Archiv für Kunst und Geschichte, Berlin	77
Couteau, Pierre	18, 24, 33, 67, 79
Henninges, Heiner / Free Lance Press	26, 40
Jung, Roland E.	10/11, 42, 49, 51, 57
Malecos, Andreas	8, 21, 60, 75
Master PhotoPress	Cover
Sierpeklis, Zenon	9
Thiele, Klaus	32, 38, 47, 61, 62, 66, 78
Thomas, Martin	3, 12, 19, 31, 43, 44 45, 48, 54, 63, 69 72/73, 76, 80, 82
Wagner, Dr. (Silvestris)	15.

INDEX

Explore the World

Nelles Maps are top quality cartography!
Relief mapping, kilometer charts and tourist attractions.
Always up-to-date!